NOT THE SCREENPLAY TO

FEAR & LOATHING

IN

LAS VEGAS

NOT THE SCREENPLAY TO

FEAR & LOATHING

IN

LAS VEGAS

BY
TERRY GILLIAM & TONY GRISONI

WITH THE COMPLETE STORYBOARDS
BY TERRY GILLIAM

APPLAUSE
NEW YORK • LONDON

AN APPLAUSE ORIGINAL

Fear and Loathing in Las Vegas: NOT The Screenplay
By Terry Gilliam and Tony Grisoni

Copyright © 1997 by Terry Gilliam & Tony Grisoni

Library of Congress Cataloguing-in-Publication Data

LC Catalog # 98-71619

British Library Cataloguing-in-Publication Data

A catalogue record for this book is available from the British Library

ISBN: 1-55783-348-9

APPLAUSE BOOKS
211 West 71st Street
New York, NY 10023
Phone: (212) 496-7511
Fax: (212) 721-2856

A&C BLACK
Howard Road
Huntington, Cambs PE19 3EZ
Phone: 0171-242-0946
Fax: 0171-831-8478

10   9   8   7   6   5   4   3   2   1

Printed in Canada

CONTENTS

Bad Credit Rating

TERRY GILLIAM

LATE MARCH 1998 . . .

I magine what it would be like to wake up one morning having spent the previous year adapting a book that had somehow managed to avoid being reduced to celluloid for over 20 years and, having gathered together a team of actors and technicians and worked for months shooting and editing the film, you are now nearing completion ... suddenly, to your horror, you are informed that you had all been working with the <u>wrong script</u>. Not the script you had co-written with Tony Grisoni, but from a script written by another director and somebody else that you don't know.

Not only that, but <u>your</u> screenplay had <u>nothing</u> to do with the film. You and Tony were to receive NO CREDIT AT ALL!!! No mention! Nada!! The credit was to read "Screenplay by Alex Cox and Tod Davies."

Hard to imagine? You bet. But this is exactly what happened when the Writers Guild of America decided to arbitrate the screenplay credits for *Fear and Loathing in Las Vegas.*

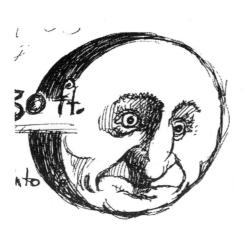

Having the world turned upside down like that could have an unsettling effect on a normal person — much less a couple of sensitive writers.

Your first thought is that <u>this is not happening</u>. It simply isn't so. You're not Joseph K. You've never had tendencies towards becoming a cockroach. Franz Kafka is definitely not alive enough to be writing this madness. Nor is Lewis Carroll. Clearly you have gone insane.

But, then you talk to the producers, the author of the original book, the actors, several independent script readers, and some psychiatrists and you are reassured that the film you are finishing has, in fact been made from the screenplay you thought you had written.

BUT WHY DON'T THE CREDITS ADMIT THIS SIMPLE TRUTH?

You now come to a terrible realization. It's not you or the rest of the world that has gone absolutely wacko, round the twist, completely out of touch with reality, but the very important organization of which you are a member — the organization that prides itself on protecting you, the writers — THE ORGANIZATION YOU HAVE BEEN GIVING 1-1/2% OF YOUR EARNING TO FOR MANY YEARS ... The Writer's Guild of America! You can imagine how disturbing this can be.

But how did this state of affairs come about?

Begin at the beginning.

One of the first things you do NOT do when you sit down to write a script is to read the small print in the massive, densely Byzantine, Writer's Guild handbook, but if you did read the small print you might discover in those murky depths that writers who are also directors are heavily discriminated against — are second class citizens.

Although we pay the same percentage of our earning to the Guild we have to produce twice as much writing to receive a credit if the script goes to arbitration ... and, if a director _is_ involved in the writing of the screenplay, it <u>automatically</u> goes to arbitration. In the language of the WGA, directors are referred to as production executives — the very people I seem to have been fighting all my life.

Now, as it happens, like many other directors, I began my film career by writing. Directing came as a way of protecting the writing — to make sure my ideas reached the screen as I intended. Yet as member of the WGA I am punished. Not only myself, but my co-writer Tony Grisoni, who is also tarred with the same brush.

Together, we have to prove that we wrote substantially more than 60% of the screenplay to receive ANY credit, any acknowledgment of our work. Another writer or team of writers needs only 33% to receive credit. The cards were stacked against us, but we had no real worries as to the extent and originality of our screenplay.

Then ... we discovered that if we included scenes from the book that were also used by writers of an earlier script they were to be credited for those scenes. They got there first. They get the points. It didn't matter if we used the scenes in a different way, in a different order, or for a different purpose. Their points! Not ours! Interesting. How is your calculator handling this?

Over the last 20-some years many screenplays have been written based on Hunter Thompson's book. They have all chosen the same basic scenes. It's the nature of the book. The first part of the book is reasonably self-evident in the way the scenes roll off the page and onto the screenplay. It is a matter of editing and choosing which dialogue to include. It's the second half that becomes more complicated — more a matter of creating a new structure, of deciding the direction the story wants to go, which scenes to incorporate, which to drop. We came up with a structure that built to a nightmarish search to understand what really happened after Raoul Duke takes "a drug too far." No one before us had handled this part of the film in this manner. We made the film darker, more disturbing. We turned Gonzo into a pagan devil. As we wrote in our deposition to the WGA. ... "Proteins are the basic building blocks of life. Depending on how they are assembled you can end up with a wombat or with Stephen Hawking. Same proteins. Different results. it's all in the way you tell it."

Well, we told it in a different way, substantially different — one that received the blessing of the great man himself, Hunter S. Thompson — unlike the previous version which had resulted in the writers beating an ignominious retreat from Hunter's house — their tales (sic) between their legs.

But I had no quarrel with them. Even if they felt that the honorable thing to do in a situation like this would be to take their names off the film (which they didn't) — the WGA would not allow it. That too is in the rule book.

The arbitration committee is composed of three WGA members, two of which have had to serve on two previous arbitrations. This is interesting because I don't know if any working writers who have ever been asked, or were able to find the time, to arbitrate — much less arbitrate twice. So who are these writers with such time on their hands? We are not able to know, nor are we able to see their reports. There is no way of knowing whether they are qualified, whether they deliberate carefully, or even bother to write a proper report.

Most of the working writers I know have been complaining about these arbitration Star Chambers for a long time, yet feel impotent to do much about the situation. They have to belong to the Guild to write for the studios. They feel they're not being judged by their peers, but by frustrated second-rate writers who have an in-built prejudice against their more successful brethren. This is an ugly accusation to make, but I am learning, the hard way, to agree with it.

There is something terribly rotten in a system that seems to rely on weights and measures, length, breadth, height ... the elements of science, commerce, surveying ... but not the elements of writing. There's an even greater rottenness when the basic rules are so discriminatory and then applied in such a slipshod way that it ends in this absurd conclusion which so completely denies reality. Using their weighing scales, for example — if it could be accurately measured that we had written 60% of the script (not substantially more, but at least 60%) and the other writers had written only 33% — then, according to the rules, they would get sole credit and we the majority writers would get zip! It makes the process, and the WGA, look utterly foolish.

The Guild claims Alex Cox and Tod Davies, and only they, have written the screenplay for our film. They have the power to make the studio use that credit on the film and all advertising or publicity. But, why does the finished film bear so little resemblance to the credited script? Where did all the new construction, dialogue, character development, extra scenes, and ideas come from?

Were these differences the result of the prop man or, perhaps, the caterers — the truth is that they <u>did</u> contribute — excellent ideas were contributed by everyone associated with this project, because that's the way we make movies. What about the new material Tony and I had been writing throughout both the shooting and post production stages of the film long after our original screenplay was finished? Had that anything to do with the final shape of the film? But, by then, my grip on reality was beginning to slip once again.

Surely, there had been a different script? One that resembled the film? The studio thought so, the production company thought so, independent experts thought so, we, the writers, thought so ... why didn't the WGA?

Perhaps there was another answer. Perhaps we were looking through the wrong end of the toilet bowl.

Let's assume, for the moment, that the Guild knows best in these matters. The studios have happily abdicated their responsibilities in these matters to the Guild, so they must know best. What if they were right? What if the other (our) screenplay was not a screenplay at all! What if, in our attempt to grapple with this important and complex book, Tony and I had not managed to write a screenplay. This would certainly be in agreement with the Guild.

Perhaps we had mistakenly created something else ... something that would provide the guidance the crew and actors would need, but was not a screenplay.

With the sudden clarity that comes from true understanding it was obvious what had happened. WE HAD CREATED A DRESS PATTERN!!!

Now everything was clear. Alex and Tod <u>had</u> written the screenplay. I, in the great tradition of all arrogant directors, <u>had completely ignored their work — treating it like shit</u> as I marched off in whatever direction my massive ego would take me. The actors and crew, in their childlike innocence, had happily whiled away the hours — cheerfully hand-crafting the film using only the finest gems from Hunter's book — as they followed (to the last gusset and tuck) <u>the beautiful and precise dress pattern that Tony and I had created</u>.

... AND WE ALL LIVED HAPPILY EVER AFTER!!! ... except for the foolish Writer's Guild who, by the time you read this, will have found themselves to be one member less.

Seeing a Pattern . . .

What was it?

A bound sheaf of around 100 typed pages: stage and camera directions interspersed with blocks of dialogue most of which was suspiciously similar to the novel, *Fear and Loathing in Las Vegas* by Hunter S. Thompson. What could it be?

Despite our own belief to the contrary, despite various readers' assertions otherwise, this was not, could not be a screenplay — at least it could not be the screenplay cast and crew imagined it to be. The Writers Guild of America had arbitrated. I knew the deal; I pay good money to this organization in return for their advice and protection. Could lessons in strict English also be an offer? And how doth the little crocodile improve his shining tail?

Curiouser and Curiouser . . .

If it wasn't a screenplay, then, what was it? What had Terry and I spent our time producing? Why had I been flown first class to Las Vegas and L.A.? What were our discussions about? The e-mails? The faxes? The so-called re-writes? What had the production company paid me to do? Obviously it had to be something beyond the Writers Guild jurisdiction.

It was a dress pattern.

Of course! All became clear. Terry Gilliam and I had created a dress pattern. I recall our first, feverish sketching of the design. We ran up a couple of sizes — tried them on. Not bad. Thank god for that fine Thompson yarn — it was worth the money; and thank god for the drugs — little did we know how much we were going to need them. The overall shape was OK, but the stitching wasn't quite right, and perhaps here was a pleat or two too many. These were details to be sorted out further down the production line. It was important to get the pattern distributed to the seamstresses, the cutters, the finishers. Each has his or her particular responsibility — their acknowledged contribution to the finished garment. That's how we do things in our trade. Credit where credit is due.

The future of bespoke tailoring.

It's a fine dress pattern and we're proud of it. And the dress has turned out well — a fine, multicolored, exuberant dress swathed in the darkest velvet. But what for the future? I have this brave-foolish notion. I want to try and write a screenplay. And if it doesn't work out, well, fuck it, there's always the schmutter trade.

Everything's got a moral, if only you can find it.

"Never imagine yourself not to be otherwise than what it might appear to others that what you were or might appear to others that what you were or might have been was not otherwise than what you had been would have appeared to them to be otherwise . . ."

I can't explain myself, because I'm not myself, you see.

— TONY GRISONI

MAKING THE SCENE — PRODUCTION SNAPSHOTS
FROM THE DESERT

PHOTOGRAPHS ON LOCATION
BY AMY GILLIAM AND PATRICK CASSAVETTI

FEAR &
LOATHING
IN
LAS VEGAS

NOT THE
SCREENPLAY

FADE IN:

A DISTINGUISHED MAN in a three-piece suit is seated behind a desk against a blank wall with one framed diploma and an American flag.

On the desk stands a framed photo of Hunter S. Thompson.

> **DISTINGUISHED MAN**
> Ladies and Gentlemen, the film you
> are about to see this evening is the
> first film ever made <u>NOT</u> based on a
> screenplay. At no time were writers
> involved. ... Efforts have been made
> to deny this astonishing, yet simple,
> truth by a dangerous, possibly for-
> eign-controlled organization which,
> for reasons of national security,
> must remain nameless ... but <u>DO</u> <u>NOT</u>
> <u>BE</u> <u>DECEIVED</u>! ... Using only the
> finest gems from the workshop of that
> great American patriot, Dr. Hunter S.
> Thompson, this film was hand-assem-
> bled by dedicated craftsmen working,
> <u>NOT</u> from a screenplay, but from an
> original and ingenious dress pattern
> designed by two fearless fighters for
> Truth, Justice and the American Way —
> Mr. Tony Grisoni and his assistant,
> Mr. Terry Gilliam. ... Remember
> Americans, do <u>NOT</u> ... I repeat ... <u>DO</u>
> <u>NOT</u> <u>BE</u> <u>DECEIVED</u>! Your country depends
> on <u>YOU</u>! Thank you.

FADE TO BLACK ...

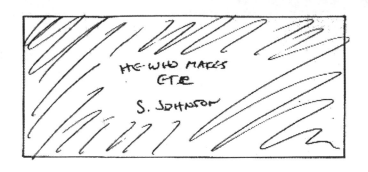

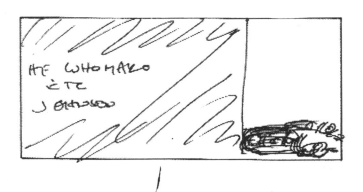

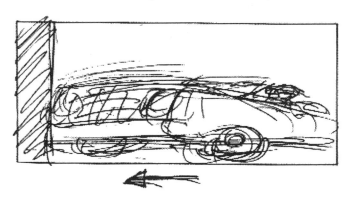

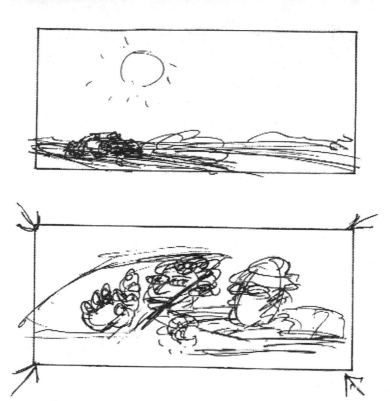

BLACK SCREEN

A desert wind moans sadly. From somewhere within the wind comes the tinkly, syrupy-sweet sounds of the Lennon Sisters singing "My Favorite Things." A series of sepia images of anti-war protests from the mid-sixties appear one after another on the screen.

In the violently scrawled style of Ralph Steadman, the title FEAR AND LOATHING IN LAS VEGAS splashes onto the screen. A beat, and then it runs down and off revealing:

TITLE: "He who makes a beast of himself
Gets rid of the pain
Of being a man."
— Dr. Johnson

The VOICE OF HUNTER S. THOMPSON — a.k.a. RAOUL DUKE:

               DUKE V/O
We were somewhere around Barstow on
the edge of the desert when the
drugs began to take hold.

3

AAAAAAAAARRRRRRRRRRRRRRRRRGGGGGGGGGGGHHHHHH!!!!!!!!

A red Chevy convertible — THE RED SHARK — wipes the black
screen.

EXT. ON THE ROAD TO LAS VEGAS — DAY

AAAAAAAAARRRRRRRRRRRRRRRRRGGGGGGGGGGGHHHHHH!!!!!!!!

THE RED SHARK races down the desert highway at a hundred
miles an hour. THE STONES' "Sympathy For the Devil"
blares.

AT THE WHEEL

STRANGELY STILL AND TENSE, RAOUL DUKE DRIVES — SKELETAL,
BEER IN HAND — STARES STRAIGHT AHEAD.

BESIDE HIM, FACE TURNED TO THE SUN, EYES CLOSED BEHIND
WRAPAROUND SPANISH SUNGLASSES, IS HIS SWARTHY AND UNNERV-
INGLY UNPREDICTABLE ATTORNEY, DR. GONZO.

The music pounds DUKE stares straight ahead. GONZO froths
up a can of beer — uses it as shaving foam.

> **DUKE V/O**
> I remember saying something like: "I
> feel a bit lightheaded. Maybe you
> should drive...."

GONZO starts shaving.

> **DUKE V/O**
> Suddenly there was a terrible roar
> all around us and the sky was full of
> what looked like huge bats, all

4

                    swooping and screeching and diving
                    around the car ...

Close on DUKE — shadows flutter across his face. The
reflections of bats swirl within his eyes. We push in
close to one eye ball — SCREECHING SWIRLING BAT-LIKE
SHAPES!

AAAAAAAARRRRRRRRRRRRRRRRGGGGGGGGGGGHHHHHH!!!!!!!!!

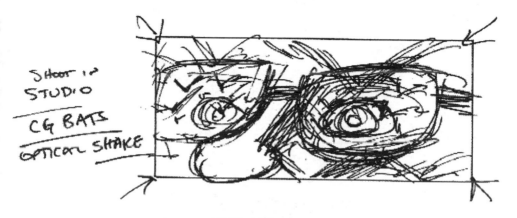

                          DUKE V/O
             ... and a voice was screaming: Holy
        Jesus! What are those goddamn ani-
        mals?

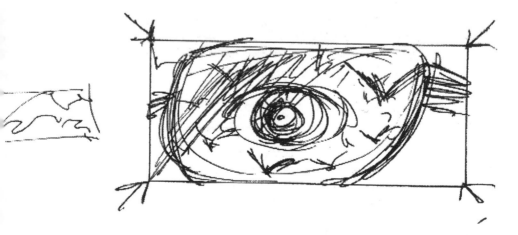

CUT TO WIDE SHOT OF CAR —

DUKE, eyes rigid, flails at the air. No bats anywhere.
GONZO casually looks over ...

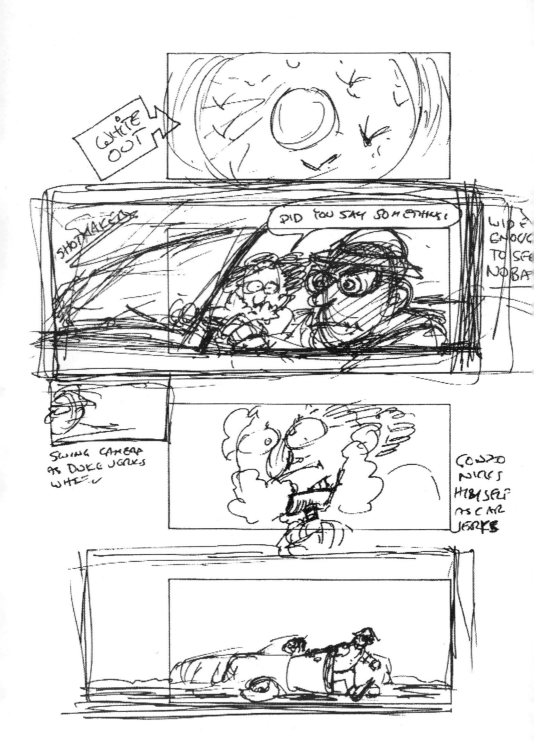

                    GONZO
        What are you yelling about?

DUKE SCREECHES to the side of the road. The sudden wrench
makes GONZO nick his face with his razor.

                    DUKE
        Never mind. It's your turn to drive.

                    DUKE V/O
        No point mentioning these bats, I
        thought. The poor bastard will see
        them soon enough.

DUKE hops out of the car, keeping an eye out for bats,
frantically opens the trunk to reveal what looks like A
MOBILE POLICE NARCOTICS LAB. DUKE desperately rifles
through the impressive stash

                    DUKE V/O
        We had two bags of grass, seventy-
        five pellets of mescaline, five
        sheets of high powered blotter acid,
        a salt shaker half full of cocaine, a
        whole galaxy of multi-colored uppers,
        downers, screamers, laughers ... Also
        a quart of tequila, a quart of rum, a
        case of beer, a pint of raw ether and
        two dozen amyls.

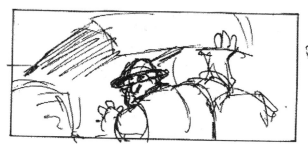

BATS?!!

DRUG
KIT

DUKE, eyes darting madly as he hears what sounds like the
SHREIKS OF BATS returning, grabs an assortment along with
another six-pack of beer — slams the trunk shut and dives
back into the car.

> **DUKE V/O**
> Not that we needed all that for the
> trip, but once you get locked into a
> serious drug collection, the tendency
> is to push it as far as you can.

THE RED SHARK RACES INTO THE DISTANCE ... on the ground,
weakly flapping is a SEMI-SQUASHED, SLOWLY DYING ANIMAL
... A BAT?

BAT THING — TIRE TRACKS

EXT. FURTHER DOWN THE ROAD TO LAS VEGAS — DAY

IN THE RED SHARK

GONZO grips the wheel — stares maniacally down the road —
a lousy driver.

> **DUKE V/O**
> The only thing that really worried me
> was the ether. There is nothing in
> the world more helpless and irrespon-
> sible and depraved than a man in the

depths of an ether binge.
And I knew we'd get into that rotten
stuff pretty soon.

The radio news wars with "SYMPATHY FOR THE DEVIL" on a
tape recorder.

RADIO NEWS
An overdose of heroin was listed as
the official cause of death for pretty 19 year old Diane Hanby whose body
was found stuffed in a refrigerator
last week....

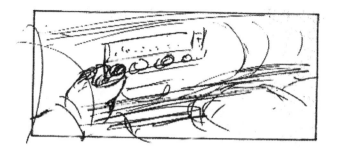

GONZO changes the station – "ONE TOKE OVER THE LINE,
SWEET JESUS, ONE TOKE OVER THE LINE" vies with "SYMPA-
THY"... He sings along — washes a couple of pills back
with a new beer. The RED SHARK fishtails.

GONZO
"One toke over the line, sweet
Jesus."

DUKE
(muttering to himself)
One toke. You poor fool. Wait till
you see those goddamn bats.

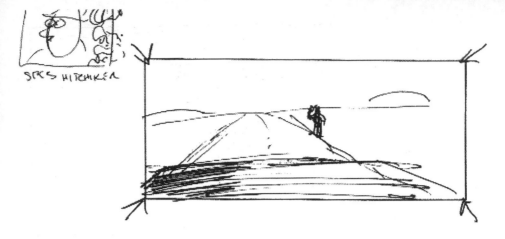

SEES HITCHHIKER

UP AHEAD — AT THE SIDE OF THE DESERTED ROAD

A LONE HITCHHIKER spots them, jumps up and sticks out a thumb. The RED SHARK roars past. Then, fifty yards down the road ...

> GONZO
> Let's give that boy a lift.

GONZO wrenches the wheel — THE RED SHARK swerves to the side of the road.

> DUKE
> We can't stop <u>here</u> — this is bat
> country!

GONZO JAMS THE CAR INTO REVERSE AND ROCKETS BACKWARDS. The HITCHHIKER races to the car. A poor OKIE KID with a big grin.

> HITCHHIKER
> Hot damn! I never rode in a convert-
> ible before!

Then the big grin freezes on the OKIE KID's face at the

10

SCREECH

CAN'T STOP
IN TIME

CRANE
DOWN

WE'RE YOUR FRIENDS!!

sight of: DUKE and GONZO looking out at him with HYPER-
NORMAL, shit-eating SMILES.

                    DUKE
          Is that right? Well, I guess you're
          about ready, eh?

The HITCHHIKER hesitates.

                    GONZO
          We're your friends. We're not like
          the others.

                    DUKE
              (hissing sharply)
          No more of that talk or I'll put the
          leeches on you.

DUKE turns back to the HITCHHIKER — smiles reassuringly.

EXT. EVEN FURTHER DOWN THE ROAD TO LAS VEGAS — DAY

The HITCHHIKER sits nervously in the back seat as the RED
SHARK screams down the road.

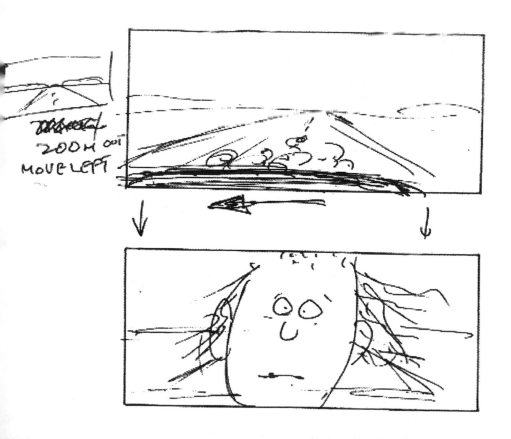

THROWING BEER CAN INTO BACK SEAT

CAN WE MAGNIFY REAR V MIRROR

GONZO sings along to the tape player.

The HITCHHIKER's eyes go to the door — considers jumping out and taking his chances

DUKE, sweating bullets, STARES AT THE HITCHHIKER in the rear view mirror.

> **DUKE V/O**
> How long could we maintain, I won-
> dered. How long before one of us
> starts raving and jabbering at this
> boy? What will he think then? This
> same lonely desert
> was the last known home of the Manson
> family.

The HITCHHIKER's eyes notice a thin line of blood trick-ling down GONZO's neck.

> **DUKE V/O**
> Would he make that grim connection
> when my attorney starts screaming
> about bats and huge manta rays coming
> down on the car?

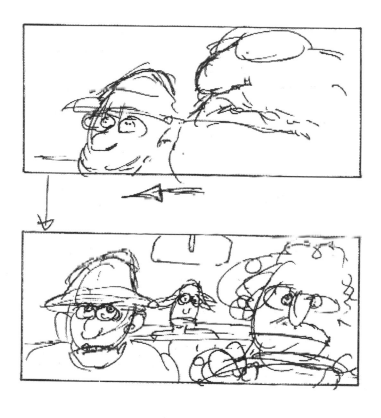

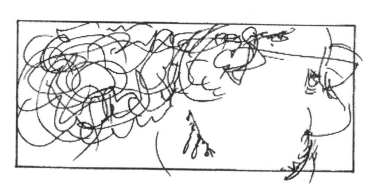

DUKE's mouth moves intermittently — sometimes in sync with the words, sometimes not.

> DUKE V/O
>
> If so — well, we'll just have to cut his head off and bury him somewhere. Because it goes without saying that we can't turn him loose. He'd report us at once to some kind of outback Nazi law enforcement agency, and they'll run us down like dogs...

> DUKE
>
> (out loud to himself)
> Jesus! Did I say that?

> DUKE V/O
>
> Or just think it? Was I talking? Did they hear me?

> GONZO
>
> (reassuringly to HITCHHIKER)
> It's okay. He's admiring the shape of your skull.

DUKE gives the HITCHHIKER a FINE BIG GRIN and the HITCH-HIKER giggles nervously.

> DUKE V/O
>
> Maybe I better have a chat with this boy I thought. Perhaps if I explain things, he'll rest easy...

> DUKE
>
> (roaring over the road
> noise)
> THERE'S ONE THING YOU SHOULD PROBABLY UNDERSTAND —

The HITCHHIKER stares at him, not blinking.

> DUKE
>
> (yells)
> CAN YOU HEAR ME?

The HITCHHIKER nods — giggles — terrified. DUKE climbs into the back seat.

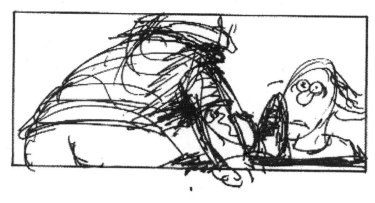

DUKE

That's good. Because I want you to
have all the background. This is a
very ominous assignment— with over-
tones of extreme personal danger. I'm
a Doctor of Journalism! This is
important, goddamnit! This is a true
story!...
    (WHACKS the BACK OF THE DRI-
        VER'S SEAT with his fist)

The CAR SWERVES SICKENINGLY, then straightens out.

> **GONZO**
> (screams)
> Keep your hands off my fucking neck!

The HITCHHIKER makes a sudden lunge for freedom. DUKE
GRABS HIM BACK DOWN.

> **DUKE V/O**
> Our vibrations were getting nasty —
> but why? Was there no communication
> in this car? Had we deteriorated to
> the level of dumb beasts?

The HITCHHIKER STRUGGLES IN PANIC.

> **DUKE**
> (to HITCHHIKER)
> I want you to understand that this
> man at the wheel is my attorney! He's
> not just some dingbat I found on the
> Strip. He's a foreigner. I think he's
> probably Samoan. But it doesn't mat-
> ter, does it? Are you prejudiced?

> **HITCHHIKER**
> Hell, no!

> **DUKE**
> I didn't think so. Because in spite
> of his race, this man is extremely
> valuable to me. Hell, I forgot all
> about this beer. You want one?
> (HITCHHIKER shakes his head)
> How about some ether?

> **HITCHHIKER**
> What?

> **DUKE**
> Never mind. Let's get right to the
> heart of this thing. Twenty-four
> hours ago we were sitting in the Pogo
> Lounge of the Beverly Wills Hotel....

INT. THE BEVERLY WILLS HOTEL POGO LOUNGE 1971 — DAY

A uniformed DWARF, carries a shockingly PINK TELEPHONE

18

through the glittering, tranquil POGO LOUNGE CROWD. They
are the ELOI. HENDRIX AFROS and DROOPING MUSTACHES and
BELL BOTTOMS and LOVE BEADS and BELLS. ACTRESSES sip
Singapore Slings and PROMOTERS sip ACTRESSES in this
MONIED, SANITISED VERSION OF THE GREAT REVOLUTION YEARS.

> ### DUKE V/O
> ... in the patio section, of course,
> drinking Singapore Slings with mescal
> on the side, hiding from the brutish
> realities of this foul year of Our
> Lord, 1971.

The DWARF reaches DUKE — T-shirt, levis, sneakers and
shades. GONZO — white rayon bellbottoms and a khaki tank
top undershirt. They are in the middle of a serious conversation.

> ### DUKE
> I'm telling you, the Salazar story is
> geting too complicated. The weasels
> have started closing in.

The DWARF sneers.

> ### DWARF
> Perhaps this is the call you've been
> waiting for all this time, sir...

DUKE lifts the receiver — listens ...

> ### DUKE
> Uh-huh.... Uh-huh.... Uh-huh....

DUKE hangs up the PHONE with the DEAD-PAN EXPRESSION OF A
MOVIE SPY.

> ### DUKE
> That was headquarters. They want me
> to go to Las Vegas at once and make
> contact with a Portuguese photograph-
> er named Lacerda. He'll have the
> details. All I have to do is check
> into my sound proof suite and he'll
> seek me out.

GONZO, says nothing for a moment, then POUNDS the table!

GONZO

God <u>hell</u>! I think I see the pattern!
This one sounds like real trouble!
You're going to need plenty of legal
advice before this thing is over.
As your attorney I must advise you
that you'll need a very fast car with
no top and after that, the cocaine.
And then the tape recorder, for special music, and some Acapulco
shirts...
> (GONZO tucks his khaki
> undershirt into his white
> bellbottoms — he means
> business!)

This blows my weekend, because natu-
rally I'll have to go with you — and
we'll have to arm ourselves.

DUKE

Why not? If a thing's worth doing,
it's worth doing right.

DUKE and GONZO are up and off. The DWARF chases after
them with the (very large) check in his hand.

They sweep out through the Lounge door, unaware of it
swinging back into the face of the pursuing DWARF

DUKE

I tell you, my man. This is the
American Dream in action! We'd be
fools not to ride this strange torpe-
do all the way out to the end.

GONZO

Indeed. We <u>must</u> do it.
What kind of story <u>is</u> this?

[SCENE 6 DELETED]

EXT. BEVERLY WILLS HOTEL — FRONT ENTRANCE — DAY

DUKE and GONZO emerge.

DUKE

The Mint 400! The richest off-road
race for motorcycles and dune-buggies

in the history of organized sport!
                    (handing parking
                    ticket to Valet)
          — a fantastic spectacle in honor of
          some fatback grossero who owns the
          luxurious Mint Hotel in the heart of
          downtown Vegas ... at least that's
          what the press release says.

Their car arrives — rusted out, smashed door panels. They
jump in.

                         DUKE
          We're going to have to drum it up on
          our own. Pure Gonzo Journalism.

And they're off in a cloud of black exhaust as the nose-
bleeding DWARF stumbles out with the unpaid bill in his
hand.

EXT. SUNSET BLVD — DAY

The PINTO races through shot.

                       DUKE V/O
          Getting hold of the drugs and shirts
          had been no problem...

EXT. POLYNESIAN BAR — DAY

The PINTO skids to a halt outside Polynesian bar, the
back window full of Hawaiian shirts.

                    DUKE V/O (cont'd)
          ... but the car and tape recorder
          were not easy things to round up at
          6:30 on a Friday afternoon in
          Hollywood.

INT. POLYNESIAN BAR — DAY

TORN YELLOW PAGES with dealer's ads ticked off lie in a
pile as GONZO yells into a PAYPHONE. DUKE carries over
four Singapore Slings.

                        GONZO
          O.K., O.K., yes. Hang onto it. We'll
          be there in thirty minutes.
                    (to DUKE — hand over the

PHONE)
I finally located a car with adequate
horsepower and the proper coloring.
                    (into PHONE)
What?! OF COURSE the gentleman has a
major credit card! Do you realize who
the fuck you're talking to?

                    DUKE
Don't take any guff from these swine.
          (GONZO slams the phone down)
Now we need a sound store with the
finest equipment. Nothing dinky. One
of those new Belgian Heliowatts with
a voice-activated shotgun mike, for
picking up conversations in oncoming
cars.

                    GONZO
We won't make the nut unless we have
unlimited credit.

                    DUKE
We will. You Samoans are all the
same. You have no faith in the essen-
tial decency of the white man's culture.

EXT. SUNSET BLVD — DUSK

The PINTO races down street

                    DUKE V/O
The store was closed, but the sales-
man said he would wait, if we hur-
ried....

EXT. SUNSET BOULEVARD — TRAFFIC JAM — DUSK

They're stuck in a traffic jam — clouds of exhaust. DUKE
BANGS ON THE HORN IN FURY.

                    DUKE V/O
But we were delayed en route when a
Stingray in front of us killed a
pedestrian.

Directly in front of them: BLOODY CARNAGE — a covered
corpse is loaded into an ambulance by PARAMEDICS.

[EXT. SOUND STORE — DUSK — OMITTED]

EXT. CAR RENTAL AGENCY — NIGHT

>   DUKE V/O
>   We had trouble, again, at the car
>   rental agency.

Behind the wheel of the RED SHARK: DUKE grins with satis-
faction — checking it out. A nervous AGENT holds out a
clipboard. DUKE signs without looking at the rental
papers.

>   AGENT
>   Say... uh... you fellas are going to
>   be careful with this car, aren't you?

>   DUKE
>   Of course.

DUKE throws the car into reverse — roars backwards past
the gas pumps to where GONZO is unloading their rusted
out car.

>   AGENT
>   Well, good god! You just backed over
>   that two foot concrete abutment and
>   you didn't even slow down! Forty-five
>   in reverse! And you barely missed the
>   pump!

>   DUKE
>   No harm done. I always test the
>   transmission that way. The rear end.
>   For stress factors.

GONZO transfers boxes of new sound equipment and a large
box of rum and ice into the RED SHARK.

>   AGENT
>   Say. Are you fellows drinking?

>   DUKE
>   Not me. We're responsible people.

He JAMS the car into LOW GEAR and lurches into traffic.
The AGENT runs into the street and helplessly watches them
go.

GONZO

There's another worrier. He's probably all cranked up on speed.

EXT. RUNDOWN BEACH HOUSE — NIGHT

STRANGE AND MAGICAL. In the moonlight: the silhouetted
figures of DUKE and GONZO as they pack the RED SHARK.

DUKE V/O

We spent the rest of that night
rounding up materials and packing the
car.
Then we ate some mescaline and went
swimming.

The surf crashes in the distance...

EXT. PACIFIC OCEAN — NIGHT

DUKE cries out as he dives into the ocean. He lets himself float up through the silvery bubbles....

DUKE AND GONZO FLOAT BEATIFICALLY IN THE GLOWING, SHIMMER-
ING MOONLIT SURF.

DUKE V/O

Our trip was different. It was to be
a classic affirmation of everything
right and true in the national character; a gross, physical salute to
the fantastic possibilities of life
in this country. But only for those
with true grit ...

EXT. AND EVEN FURTHER DOWN THE ROAD TO LAS VEGAS — DAY

DUKE's intense face.

> **DUKE**
> ... and we're chock full of that!

> **GONZO**
> Damn right!

> **DUKE**
> My attorney understands this concept,
> despite his racial handicap. But do
> you?!

The HITCHHIKER nods — giggles — petrified.

> **DUKE V/O**
> He <u>said</u> he understood, but I could
> see in his eyes that he didn't. He
> was lying to me.

> **GONZO**
> My heart!

GONZO clutches his heart. The car veers off the road and
screeches to a halt. He slumps over the wheel.

                    GONZO (CONT'D)
             Where's the medicine?

                         DUKE
             The medicine? Yes, it's right here.

DUKE spills out 4 AMYL CAPSULES from a tin.

                         DUKE
             Don't worry, this man has a bad
             heart... Angina Pectoris. But we have
             a cure for it.

DUKE and GONZO break 2 AMYLS apiece — INHALE DEEPLY.
GONZO falls back on the seat, staring straight up at the
sun. The HITCHHIKER looks petrified.

                        GONZO
                (Suddenly flailing his naked
                    arms at the sky)
             Turn up the fucking music! My heart
             feels like an alligator! Volume!
             Clarity! Bass! We must have bass!
             What's wrong with us? Are we goddamn
             old ladies?

                         DUKE
                (Turns up music to
                    full volume)
             You scurvy shyster bastard! Watch
             your language! You're talking to a
             Doctor of Journalism!

                        GONZO
                (Laughing uncontrollably)
             What the fuck are we doing out here?
             Somebody call the police! We need
             help!

                         DUKE
                (to HITCHHIKER)
             Pay no attention to this swine. He
             can't handle the medicine.
                (he begins laughing)

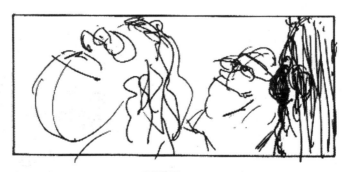

GONZO
(to the HITCHHIKER)
The truth is we're going to Vegas to
croak a scag baron named Savage
Henry. I've known him for years but
he ripped us off — and you know what
that means, right?

GONZO pulls out a .357 Magnum — waves it around.

GONZO (CONT'D)
Savage Henry has cashed his check!
We're going to rip his lungs out!

DUKE
TAKES
HAT OFF."
PUTS ARM
AROUND
HITCHHIKE

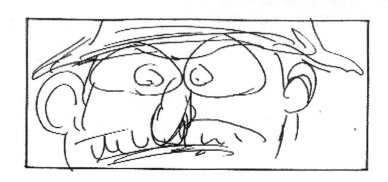

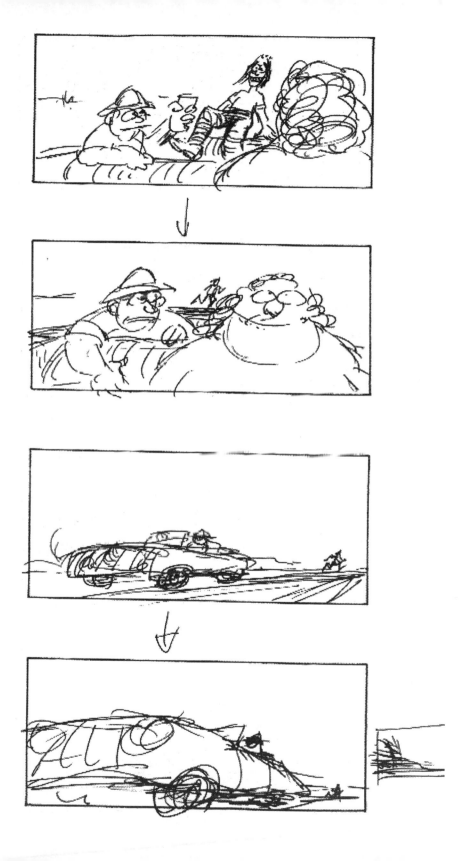

                    DUKE
        And eat them! That bastard won't get
        away with this! What's going on in
        this country when a scum sucker like
        that can get away with sandbagging a
        Doctor of Journalism?

GONZO cracks ANOTHER AMYL.

The HITCHHIKER SCRAMBLES OUT OF THE CAR, DOWN THE TRUNK
LID, AND FLEES.

                  HITCHHIKER
        Thanks for the ride. Thanks a lot. I
        like you guys. Don't worry about me.

                    DUKE
                  (yells)
        Wait a minute! Come back and have a
        beer!

The HITCHHIKER RUNS from car.

                  GONZO
        Good riddance. That boy made me ner-

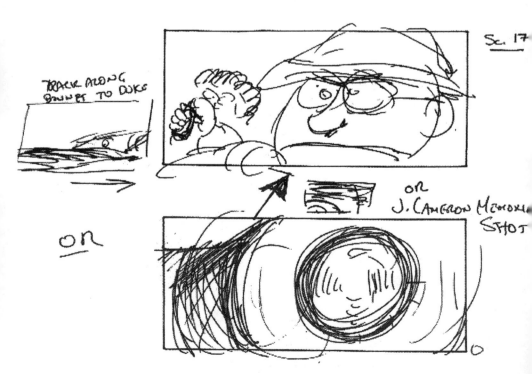

vous. Did you see his eyes?
                    (laughing)
Jesus, this is good medicine!

DUKE glances back at the running HITCHHIKER.

                    DUKE
            (suddenly clambering into
              the front seat)
Move over!! We have to get out of
California before that kid finds a
cop!

DUKE GUNS THE RED SHARK — TAKES OFF DOWN THE ROAD...

EXT. UNBELIEVABLY FAR DOWN THE ROAD TO LAS VEGAS — DAY

THE RED SHARK races — DUKE at the wheel — straight ahead
driving.

                    DUKE V/O
It was absolutely imperative that we
get to the Mint Hotel before the
deadline for press registration.
Otherwise, we might have to pay for
our suite.

GONZO wrestles with a shaker of COCAINE. The top comes
off and the powder swirls away on the wind.

                    GONZO
Oh, Jesus! Did you see what god just
did to us?

                    DUKE
God didn't do that! You did it!
You're a fucking narcotics agent,
that was our cocaine, you pig!

                    GONZO
            (waving the .357 Magnum
              at Duke)
You better be careful. Plenty of vul-
tures out here. They'll pick your
bones clean before morning.

                    DUKE
You whore!

GONZO tears up a BLOTTER OF ACID.

> **GONZO**
> Here — chew this. It's your half of
> the acid.

DUKE takes his half — chews it.

> **DUKE**
> How long do I have?

> **GONZO**
> Maybe thirty more minutes. As your
> attorney, I advise you to drive at
> top speed. It'll be a goddamn miracle
> if we can get there before you turn
> into a wild animal. Are you ready for
> that? Checking into a Vegas hotel
> under a phony name with intent to
> commit capital fraud and a head full
> of acid.

> **DUKE V/O**
> Thirty minutes. It was going to be
> very close.

The RED SHARK screams along the highway past a billboard:
"DON'T GAMBLE WITH MARIJUANA! \ IN NEVADA: POSSESSION — 20
YEARS; SALE — LIFE!!"

EXT. LAS VEGAS MINT HOTEL — DUSK

The RED SHARK pulls up outside the MINT. A great banner
spanning the street announces the MINT 400.

DUKE can feel the drug surging up inside him. Clutching a
buckled beer can, sweat pouring, he stares fixedly at the
TICKET the ATTENDANT gives him.

DUKE

I need this, right?

ATTENDANT

I'll remember your face.

DUKE stares — losing it...

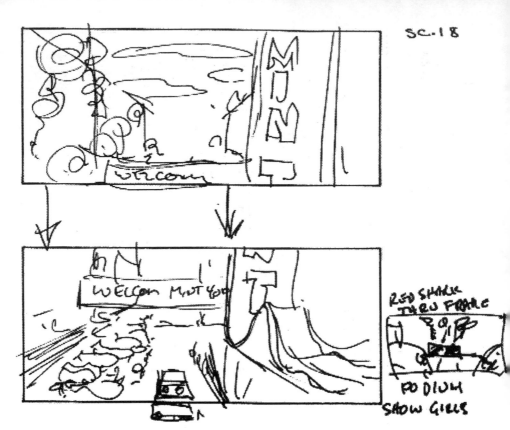

RED SHARK
THRU FRAME

PODIUM
SHOW GIRLS

                    DUKE V/O
          There is no way of explaining the
          terror I felt.

INT. HOTEL LOBBY — DAY

DUKE waits in line at the front desk — RIGID WITH PENT UP
ENERGY. GONZO's ahead of him — muscling in — trying to
queue jump and failing.

                    DUKE V/O
          I was pouring sweat. My blood is too
          thick for Nevada. I've never been
          able to properly explain myself in
          this climate.

A COUPLE move off and DUKE jerks forward — stops — eyes
fixed on the stony FEMALE RESERVATIONS CLERK.

                DUKE V/O (CONT'D)
          Be quiet, be calm ... name, rank, and
          press affiliation, nothing else ...

DUKE moves ANOTHER RIGID STEP CLOSER to the desk — the

Sc 19

16 m~

12 m~

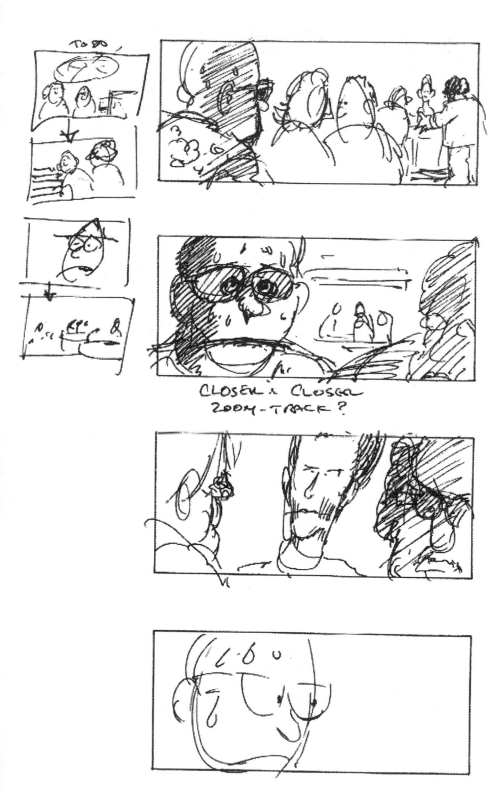

TILT
DOWN/
LOCK
OFF

CARPET PULSATING

CARPET CRAWLING UP WALL & LEG

CRANE UP - TRACK ZOOM GOING WIDE

- NO
GONZO

CRANE DOWN

NECK SWELLS   —   SCARF FLAPS INTO SHOT

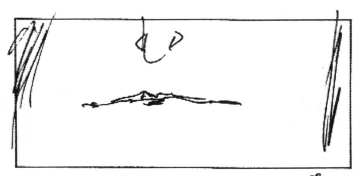

EYES GET TINY — MIGRATE APART

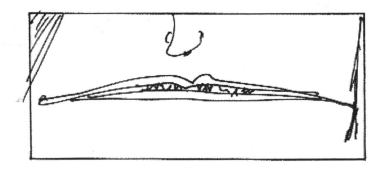

MOUTH WIDENS / GLIMPSE of RAZOR TEETH

SWELLING NECK
& MORPH   SCARF

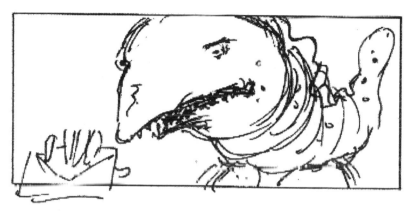

tension almost snapping him in two. GONZO's FLAPPING
AROUND — absolutely no success.

Something catches DUKE's eye... He REMAINS ROOTED — his
eyes turning to the VEGETAL PAISLEY PATTERNS ON THE CARPET
WHICH ARE SHIFTING — UNDULATING. THE CARPET PATTERNS ARE
INEXORABLY CREEPING UP THE WALLS...

> **DUKE V/O (CONT'D)**
> ... ignore this terrible drug, pre-
> tend it's not happening....

The LAST PEOPLE leave — with A FINAL, STIFF MOVE, DUKE
comes face to face with the RESERVATIONS CLERK ... AND
EXPLODES!

> **DUKE**
> HI THERE. MY NAME ... AH, RAOUL DUKE
> ... ON ... ON THAT LIST, THAT'S FOR
> SURE. FREE LUNCH, FINAL WISDOM, TOTAL
> COVERAGE ... WHY NOT? I HAVE MY
> ATTORNEY WITH ME, AND I REALIZE OF
> COURSE ...

As DUKE stares at her, BABBLING, her FACE BEGINS TO
MORPH. He tries to stop it happening by TALKING FASTER.

> **DUKE**
> ... THAT HIS NAME IS NOT ON THE
> LIST, BUT WE MUST HAVE THAT SUITE.
> YES. JUST CHECK THE LIST AND YOU'LL
> SEE. DON'T WORRY. WHAT'S THE SCORE
> HERE? WHAT'S NEXT?

DUKE sags — grips the desk — WHITE KNUCKLES.

> **RESERVATIONS CLERK**
> (hands him an envelope)
> Your suite's not ready yet. But
> there's somebody looking for you.

Her face is CHANGING — SWELLING — PULSING ...

> **DUKE**
> (shouts)
> NO! WHY? WE HAVEN'T <u>DONE</u> ANYTHING
> YET!

The FACE OF THE RESERVATIONS CLERK TURNS GREEN & GROWS

FANGS. DEADLY POISON! DUKE LUNGES BACK at GONZO, who GRIPS
his arm intensely — REACHES OUT to take the ENVELOPE.

> **GONZO**
> I can handle this. This man has a bad
> heart, but I have plenty of medicine.
> My name is Dr. Gonzo. Prepare our
> suite at once. We'll be in the bar.

GONZO manoeuvres DUKE away from the desk. DUKE looks back
— the RESERVATIONS CLERKS is now a MORAY EEL — green
jowls and fangs.

INT NAUTICAL BAR — DAY

The bar — OILY PEOPLE — quiet music — nautical theme.
DUKE and GONZO at the bar, a marlin spike hanging on the
wall behind them. DUKE has turned to stone....

> **GONZO**
> (to the bartender)
> Two Cuba Libres with beer and mescal
> on the side.
> (opens the envelope)
> Who's Lacerda, he's waiting for us in
> a room on the twelfth floor?

> **DUKE**
> Lacerda?

> **DUKE V/O**
> I couldn't remember. The name rang a
> bell, but I couldn't concentrate.
> Terrible things were happening all
> around us....

DUKE is staring — RAPT — TERRIFIED. BLOOD FLOWS FREELY
onto the floor. DUKE keeps his voice low.

> **DUKE**
> Order some golf shoes. Otherwise,
> we'll never get out of this place
> alive. It's impossible to walk in
> this muck — no footing at all ...

DUKE looks up — GONZO has disappeared.

DUKE looks around him — the entire room has TRANSFORMED
into a ROOM FILLED WITH REPTILES IN CLOTHES, DRINKING AND

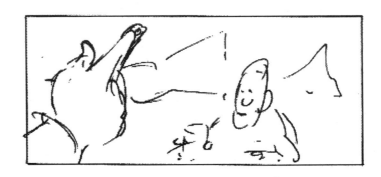

DAN ACROSS ROOM

NUTS TO BUGS

REPTILE TONGUE SNAPS UP BUGS

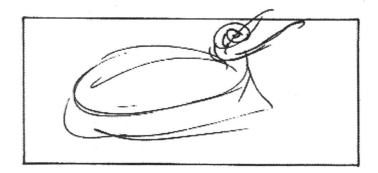

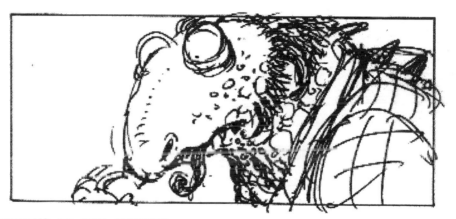

GNAWING AT ONE ANOTHER.

>   DUKE V/O
>   I was right in the middle of a fuck-
>   ing reptile zoo. And somebody was
>   giving booze to these goddamn things!
>   It won't be long before they tear us
>   to shreds!

GONZO IS SUDDENLY BACK — AT DUKE'S SHOULDER.

>   GONZO
>   If you think we're in trouble now
>   wait until you see what's happening
>   in the elevators.

GONZO removes his sunshades and we see he's been crying...as he speaks he seems to be floating. Duke struggles
to keep him in his line of vision.

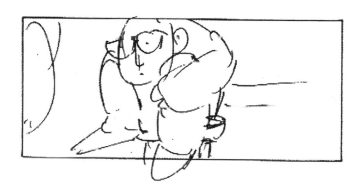

BLOOD COVERING FLOOR

IF YOU THINK WE'RE IN TROUBLE NOW..

I JUST
WENT UPSTAIRS
TO SEE
THIS MAN
LACERDA

ROOM & GONZO TURN

BUT WHEN
I MENTIONED
SAVAGE HENRY

~~EITHER~~ GONZO'S GONZO'S MOUTH ARE FLOATING
THRU FRAME

HE
KNOWS
WE'RE
ON TO
HIM

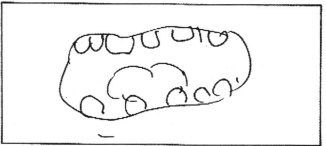

TRYING TO HOLD GONZO FROM FLOATING

BUT WHAT ABOUT OUR ROOM?
AND THE GOLF SHOES

PIECES OF MEAT

BLOOD

SEVERED TAIL

AL

HOLY SHIT: THEY'VE SPOTTED US!

THATS THE PRESS TABLE ...

YOU HANDLE THAT

DUKE SCRAMBLES ONTO BAR

MARLIN IN BACKGROUND

GONZO
     I just went upstairs to see this man
     Lacerda. I told him I knew what he
     was up to....
               (GONZO rallies — turns
                fierce)
     He says he's a photographer! But when
     I mentioned Savage Henry he freaked!
     He knows we're onto him!

                    DUKE
     But what about our room? And the golf
     shoes?

A GROUP OF REPTILES AT A TABLE ACROSS THE ROOM stares at
them, BLOOD DRIPPING FROM THEIR FANGS.

                DUKE (CONT'D)
          (grabbing GONZO trying to
           hold him still)
     Holy shit! Look at that bunch over
     there! They've spotted us!

Cut to wider shot — DUKE is holding on to a man standing
next to him at the bar. The room has returned to normality. GONZO is sitting in his original position.

                    GONZO
          (downs his drink — gets up)
     That's the press table. Where you
     have to sign in for our credentials.
     Shit, let's get it over with. You
     handle that, and I'll check on the
     room.

                    DUKE
     No, no. Don't leave me!

Black screen.

INT. MINT HOTEL SUITE — DUSK

A TELEVISION shows the NIGHTLY NEWS. A BUDDHIST MONK,
protesting the war, sets himself on fire. A very nervous
BELL BOY is laying out GONZO's order.A marlin spike is on
the floor next to DUKE.

54

BELL BOY
Four club sandwiches, four shrimp
cocktails.

DUKE
There's a big ...machine in the sky
... some kind of electric snake ...

DUKE is curled by the window — MESMERIZED by an unseen
neon sign outside the window. His eyes fill with a mil-
lion colored lights.

BELL BOY
... a quart of rum ...

DUKE
... coming straight at us.

GONZO
Shoot it.

DUKE
Not yet. I want to study its habits.

BELL BOY
... and nine fresh grapefruit.

GONZO
Vitamin C. We'll need all we can get.

GONZO sees the BELL BOY out the door — turns and lays
into DUKE.

GONZO
Look, you've got to stop this talk
about snakes and leeches and lizards
and that stuff. It's making me sick!

DUKE stares — hears the drone of B52 BOMBERS....

On TV: The LAOS INVASION — A SERIES OF HORRIFYING DISAS-
TERS — EXPLOSIONS AND TWISTED WRECKAGE.

Newsreel footage of MAI LAI MASSACRE and the LIEUTENANT
CALLEY court-martial.

DUKE
What are you talking about?

GONZO
You bastard! They'll never let us
back in that place. I leave you alone
for three minutes and you start waving that goddamn marlin spike around
— yelling about reptiles! You scared
the shit out of those people! They
were ready to call the cops. Hell,
the only reason they gave us press
passes was to get you out of
there....

A knock at the door. DUKE and GONZO break out in a sweat.

DUKE
Oh my God! Who's that?!

GONZO STICKS HIS GUN IN HIS WAISTBAND — opens the door to
LACERDA — BOUNCING WITH PUPPY DOG ENTHUSIASM. GONZO stares
at a man he instantly hates — watches him with deep sus-
picion.

LACERDA
Duke? I'm Lacerda your photographer.
Got your press passes? Good, good.

IF POSSIBLE GET AERIAL FOOTAGE
OF FLEEING PEASANTS

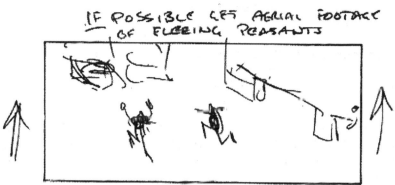

Too bad you missed the bikes checking
in. My, what a sight!

DUKE watches the B-52S DROP THEIR BOMB LOADS.

Looking down to the thick, patterned carpet, DUKE sees the
BOMBS EXPLODE like vicious flowers.

DUKE looks up: LACERDA is a war photographer — bruised,
filthy and blood spattered. LACERDA approaches him — talking a foreign language.

> **LACERDA**
> Husquavarnas. Yamahas. Kawaskis.
> Maicos. Pursang. Swedish Fireballs.
> Couple of Triumphs, here and there a
> CZ. All very fast. What a race it's
> gonna be.

DUKE screws up his eyes — WILLS NORMALITY BACK. LACERDA
is now just a keen photographer.

> **LACERDA**
> Well, we start at dawn. Get a good
> night's sleep. I know I will.

And with a cheerful wave, he's gone. DUKE is in shock.

                              DUKE
                          (weakly)
                    That's good....

                              GONZO
                    I think he's lying to us. I could see
                    it in his eyes.

                              DUKE
                          (even weaker)
                    They'll probably have a big net for
                    us when we show up.

DUKE's attention returns to the devastation on the TV ...

                              GONZO
                    Turn that shit off!

GONZO kills the TV.

Black screen.

                              DUKE V/O
                    Never lose sight of the primary
                    responsibility. Cover the story.But
                    what was the story? Nobody had both-
                    ered to say.

EXT. DESERT — DAWN

Against A BIG ORANGE SUN,on a concrete slab, MEN FIRE
SHOTGUNS into the dawn sky. Clay pigeons shatter. The Mint
Gun Club.

Next to them, MOTORCYCLES REV — preparing for the MINT
400 RACE: A hundred BIKERS, MECHANICS and assorted MOTOR-
SPORT TYPES milling around in the pit area; taping head-
lights, topping off oil in the forks, last minute bolt
tightening.

DUKE wanders through.

                              DUKE V/O
                    The racers were ready at dawn. Very
                    tense. But the race didn't start
                    until nine so we had three long hours
                    to kill.

A sign by a long trestle table: "KOFFEE & DONUTS". DUKE

walks past — ignores the SMILING LADY behind the stall.

> ### DUKE V/O (CONT'D)
> Those of us who had been up all night
> were in no mood for coffee and
> donuts. We wanted strong drink. We
> were, after all, the Absolute Cream
> of the National Sporting Press and we
> were gathered here, in Las Vegas, for
> a very special assignment. And when
> it comes to things like this you
> don't fool around.

INT. RACE BAR TENT — DAY

A real pit of iniquity Slot Machines. Crap tables. Smoke.
Drunken shouting. The absolute cream of the NATIONAL
SPORTING PRESS.

DUKE is at the bar, engaged in drunken conversation with
a LIFE REPORTER..showing him his notebook.

> ### DUKE
> See..."Kill the body and the head
> will die"...the Frazier/Ali fight....

> ### MAGAZINE REPORTER
> A proper end to the 60's ... Ali
> beaten by a human hamburger!

> ### DUKE
> And both Kennedy's murdered by
> mutants.

A SHOUT goes up from outside. The sound of engines
revving.

> ### A REPORTER
> That's it! They're starting!

In a sudden rush the PRESS CROWD make for the door taking
DUKE with them.

EXT. DESERT — DAY

MOTORCYCLES REV — tension builds...

A flag goes down. The CROWD cheers. The MOTORCYCLES ROAR
AWAY. A great cloud of dust goes up — obscuring the RAC-

ERS as they disappear into the desert ...

A moment ...

A REPORTER
> Well, that's that. They'll be back in
> an hour or so. Let's go back to the
> bar.

The CROWD turns and streams back into the tent.

INT. RACE BAR TENT — DAY

DUKE heads for the bar along with the REST. It's packed.
Drinks are ordered.

A shout from outside the tent goes up:

VOICE OFF
> Group 2!

The CROWD rushes for the door. DUKE gets swept along.

EXT. DESERT — DAY

MOTORCYCLES REV. A flag goes down. The CROWD cheers. The
MOTORCYCLES ROAR AWAY. Another great cloud of dust goes
up....

The CROWD head back for the bar.

INT. RACE BAR TENT — DAY

The CROWD surge back to the bar.

VOICE OFF
> Group 3!

This time DUKE fights his way free of the CROWD.

DUKE V/O
> There was something like 190 more
> bikes waiting to start. They were due
> to go off 10 at a time every 2 min-
> utes.

DUKE hits the bar.

DUKE
> Beer!

A middle-aged HOODLUM in a T-shirt booms up to the bar.

                    HOODLUM
          God damn! What day is this —
          Saturday?

                    DUKE
          More like Sunday.

                    HOODLUM
          Hah! That's a bitch, ain't it? Last
          night I was home in Long Beach and
          somebody said they were runnin' the
          Mint 400 today, so I says to my old
          lady, "Man, I'm goin'." So she gives
          me a lot of crap about it, so I start
          slappin' her around, and the next
          thing you know two guys I never seen
          before are beating me stupid.

                    VOICE OFF
          Group 4!

Outside, another batch of motorcycles roar away — kicking
up more clouds of dust.

                    HOODLUM
          Then they gave me ten bucks, put me
          on a bus, and when I woke up here I
          was in downtown Vegas, and for a
          minute all I could think was, "O
          Jesus, who's divorcing me this time?"
          But then I remembered, by God! I was
          here for the Mint 400. And, man, I
          tell you, it's wonderful to be here.
          Just wonderful to be here with you
          people.

A silence. A MAGAZINE REPORTER lunges across the bar —
grabs the BARTENDER.

                    MAGAZINE REPORTER
          Senzaman wassyneeds!

                    DUKE
                    (smacks the bar with his
                     palm)
          Hell yes! Bring us ten!

                          61

                        VOICE OFF
          Group 5!

                    MAGAZINE REPORTER
                        (screams)
          I'll back it!
                (slides off his stool to the
                        floor)

          Outside, motorcycles roar away. The dust cloud billows
          into the tent — getting denser.

                  MAGAZINE REPORTER (CONT'D)
                      (on the floor)
          This is a magic moment in sport! It
          may never come again! I once did the
          Triple Crown, but it was nothing like
          this.

          A FROG-EYED WOMAN claws at the MAGAZINE REPORTER, tries to
          haul him up.

                      FROG-EYED WOMAN
          Please stand up! You're a correspon-
          dent for a major national magazine
          who's name we can't get clearance
          for! Please! You'd be a very handsome
          man if you'd just stand up!

                    MAGAZINE REPORTER
          Listen, madam. I'm damn near intoler-
          ably handsome down here where I am.
          You'd go crazy if I stood up!

          A feverishly eager LACERDA appears out of the dust cloud,
          3 cameras slung round his neck.

                        LACERDA
          Club soda, please.

                      FROG-EYED WOMAN
                    (to MAGAZINE REPORTER)
          Please! I love Life!

                        LACERDA
                        (to DUKE)
          Man, it's great out there!

                              DUKE
          Lunatics.

LACERDA grins.

                           VOICE OFF
             Group 6!

                            LACERDA
          Meet you outside!

LACERDA downs his drink — hurries out through the crowd
and out into the cloud of dust.

EXT. DESERT — DAY

Nothing. Except for a THICK CLOUD OF DUST.

Barely visible, a motorcycle comes speeding into the pits.
The RIDER staggers off his bike. The PIT CREW gas it up
and sends it back with a FRESH RIDER.

DUKE watches him disappear back into the dust cloud.

                          DUKE V/O
             By 10 they were spread out all over
             the course. It was no longer a race,
             now it was an Endurance Contest. The
             idea of trying to "cover this race"
             in any conventional press sense was
             absurd.

A HORN HONKS. A shiny BLACK BRONCO with DRIVER. LACERDA
hangs out of the window.

                            LACERDA
             It's great, isn't it?! Jump in!

DUKE gets into the Bronco and they head into the DUST
CLOUD.

EXT. DESERT — DAY

IN THE BRONCO.

DUKE hangs on with his beer. Nothing all around but the
HUGE IMPENETRABLE CLOUD OF DUST. LACERDA snaps madly away
at nothing at all!

> LACERDA
>
> I'll just keep trying different com-
> bos of film and lenses till I find
> one that works in this dust!

The SOUND OF MOTORCYCLES RACING ...

We hear music and voices singing:

> BATTLE HYMN
>
> "...As we go marching on
> When I reach my final campground, in
> that land beyond the sun,
> And the Great Commander asks me..."
> (What did he ask you, Rusty?)
> "Did you fight or did you run?"
> A moment later, the Bronco races out
> of the dust. DUKE coughs, chokes,
> drinks beer.

> BATTLE HYMN
> (continuing)
> (And what did you tell them, Rusty?)
> "We responded to their rifle fire
> with everything we had..."

The sound of gun shots...

A DUNE BUGGY races toward them, loaded down with THREE
RETIRED PETTY OFFICERS, DRUNK AS HELL. The radio blares:
"THE BATTLE HYMN OF LIEUTENANT CALLEY".

The dune buggy is COVERED WITH OMINOUS SYMBOLS: SCREAMING
EAGLES CARRYING AMERICAN FLAGS IN THEIR CLAWS. A slant-
eyed Snake being chopped to bits by a buzz-saw made of
stars and stripes. A MACHINE GUN MOUNT on the passenger
side. They yell over the roaring engines.

> DUNE BUGGY DRIVER
> Where's the damn race?

> DUKE
> Beats me. We're just good patriotic
> Americans like yourself.

DUKE gives DUNE BUGGY PASSENGER #2 A NICE BIG GRIN. In
response, the PASSENGER #2 narrows his eyes — tightens his
grip on an automatic weapon.

                    DUNE BUGGY DRIVER
                     (suspiciously)
              What outfit you fellas with?

                          DUKE
              The sporting press. We're friendlies.
              Hired geeks.

The DRIVER and DUNE BUGGY PASSENGER #2 exchange looks.

                          DUKE
              If you want a good chase, you should
              get after that skunk from CBS News up
              ahead in the black jeep. He's the man
              responsible for that book, THE SELL-
              ING OF THE PENTAGON.

                    DUNE BUGGY PASSENGER #1
              HOT DAMN!

                    DUNE BUGGY PASSENGER #2
              A black jeep, you say?

And they ROAR away.

                          DUKE
              Take me back to the pits.

                        LACERDA
              No, no - we have to go on. We need
              total coverage.

DUKE gets out of the Bronco.

                          DUKE
              You're _fired_.

After a moment's hesitation, LACERDA and the BRONCO driver
roar away leaving DUKE alone in the cloud of dust.

                        DUKE V/O
              It was time, I felt, for an Agonizing
              Reappraisal of the whole scene. The
              race was definitely under way. I had
              witnessed the start; I was sure of
              that much. But what now?

EXT. LAS VEGAS STREETS — NIGHT

MUSIC PUMPS OUT. CRUISING IN THE RED SHARK IN VEGAS. THE
SKY SWIRLS WITH MILLIONS OF NEON LIGHTS CHASING EACH OTHER
IN BAROQUE PATTERNS ACROSS GIGANTIC HOTEL SIGNS.
PSYCHEDELIC LIGHT SHOWS TO LURE AND DERANGE THE INNOCENT.
CITY OF LOST SOULS.

> ### DUKE
> Turn up the radio! Turn up the tape
> machine! Roll the windows down. Let's
> taste this cool desert wind! Aaah,
> yes! This is what it's all about!

DUKE, beer in hand, drives — a big smile for the world.
GONZO scans The Vegas Visitor.

> ### DUKE V/O
> Total control now. Tooling along the
> main drag on a Saturday night in
> Vegas, two good old boys in a fire
> apple red convertible ... stoned,
> ripped, twisted ... Good people!

> ### GONZO
> How about "Nickel Nick's Slot
> Arcade"? "Hot Slots," that sounds
> heavy. Twenty-nine cent hotdogs ...

> ### DUKE
> Look,what are we doing here? Are we
> here to entertain ourselves, or to <u>do
> the job?</u>

> ### GONZO
> To do the job, of course. Here we go
> .. a Crab Louie and quart of muscatel
> for twenty dollars!

The Shark hits a bump.

> ### GONZO
> As your attorney I advise you to
> drive over to the Tropicana and pick
> up on Guy Lombardo. He's in the Blue
> Room with his Royal Canadians.

They hit another bump.

                    DUKE
    Why?

                    GONZO
    Why what?

CUT to wide shot. They are DRIVING AROUND IN CIRCLES in a
large casino parking lot, bumping over the dividers.

                    DUKE
    Why should I pay out my hard-earned
    dollars to watch a fucking corpse. I
    don't know about you, but in my line

Sc 31

    of business it's important to be Hep.

EXT. DESERT ROOM HOTEL — NIGHT

TWO BIG SCREAMING FACES.

                    DOORMAN 1
    What the hell are you doing?!

Sc 31

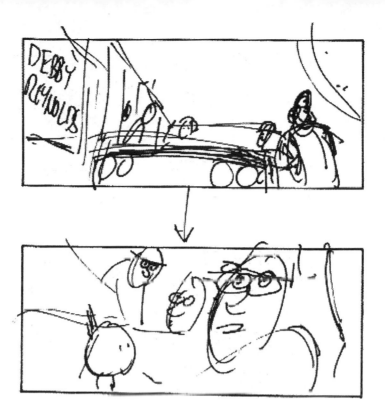

DOORMAN 2
You can't park <u>here</u>!

DUKE
Why not? Is this not a reasonable
place to park?

Reveal the RED SHARK parked on the sidewalk in front of
the Desert Inn. TWO DOORMEN loom over the car hood. The
MARQUEE says: TONIGHT. DEBBIE REYNOLDS.

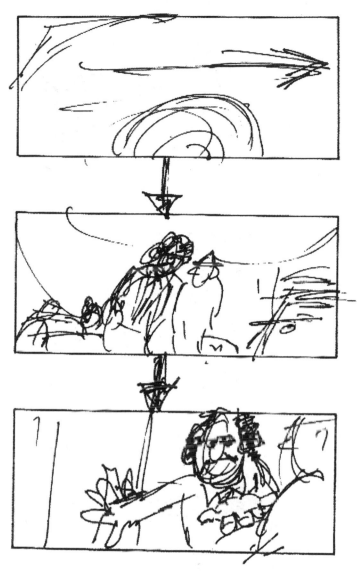

GONZO leaps from the car, waving a five-dollar bill at
the DOORMAN.

GONZO

> We want this car parked! We drove all
> the way from L.A. for this show.
> We're friends of Debbie's.

A pause, then ... the DOORMAN pockets the bill, hands
them a parking stub. DUKE and GONZO hurry into the hotel.

INT. DESERT ROOM HOTEL LOBBY — NIGHT

DUKE and GONZO walk through the lobby. Black, mirrored,

sleek, classy.

>   **DUKE**
>   Holy shit! They almost had us there!
>   That was quick thinking.

>   **GONZO**
>   What do you expect? I'm your
>   <u>attorney</u>. You owe me five bucks. I
>   want it now.

DUKE shrugs and hands over the $5

>   **DUKE V/O**
>   This was Bob Hope's turf. Frank
>   Sinatra's. Spiro Agnew's. It seemed
>   inappropriate to be haggling about
>   nickel/dime bribes for the parking
>   lot attendant.

A WINE-COLORED TUXEDO stops them at the entrance to the ballroom.

>   **WINE-COLORED TUXEDO**
>   Sorry, full house.

>   **GONZO**
>   Goddamnit, we drove all the way from
>   L.A.

>   **WINE-COLORED TUXEDO**
>   I said there are no seats left..at
>   any price.

>   **GONZO**
>   Fuck seats! We're old friends of
>   Debbie's. I used to <u>romp</u> with her.

GONZO and the WINE-COLORED TUXEDO get into an ugly arm-waving negotiation.

>   **DUKE V/O**
>   After a lot of bad noise, he let us
>   in for nothing provided we would
>   stand quietly at the back and not
>   smoke.

As DUKE and GONZO disappear through the door we can hear the orchestra blasting out a HIGHLY BLANDIZED "SGT. PEP-

PER'S LONELY HEARTS CLUB BAND."

A beat.

The door flies open and BOUNCERS manhandle DUKE and GONZO
out. Despite the rough treatment they're both SCREECHING
WITH LAUGHTER.

                          GONZO
              Jesus creeping shit!

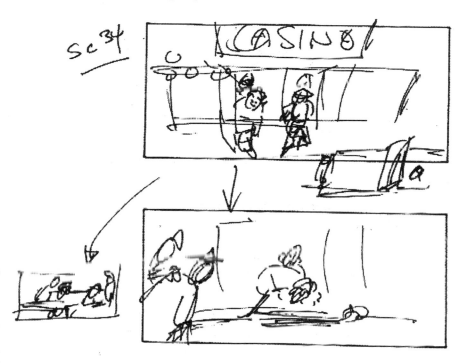

                          DUKE
                    (tears streaming)
              Did the mescaline just kick in? Or
              was that Debbie Reynolds in a silver
              Afro wig?!

                          GONZO
                    (in hysteria)
              We wandered into a fucking time cap-
              sule!

[OMITTED

EXT. DESERT ROOM — NIGHT

OMITTED

EXT. LAS VEGAS STREETS — NIGHTS]

EXT. LAS VEGAS STREETS — NIGHT

DUKE DRIVES FAST into the night. They're both LAUGHING
HYSTERICALLY.

                    DUKE
              (in hysteria)
         We wandered into a fucking time cap-
         sule!

THEN ... GONZO finds a TINY TEAR IN HIS JACKET ...

                   GONZO
         What's this?...

GONZO is instantly MOROSE.

                   GONZO
         That scum ...

GONZO twists round in the car - SCREAMS back into the
night.

                   GONZO
         SCUM! I know where you live! I'll
         find you and burn down your fucking
         house!

EXT. BAZOOKO CIRCUS — NIGHT

A hundred foot high neon clown: BAZOOKO CIRCUS.

The RED SHARK pulls up beneath the sign.

                    DUKE
         This is the place. They'll never fuck
         with us here.

                   GONZO
         Where's the ether? This mescaline
         isn't working.

EXT. BAZOOKO CIRCUS CASINO — NIGHT

Into the GLARING, CHASING LIGHTS of the entrance canopy
steps DUKE in EC/U holding a KLEENEX SOAKED IN ETHER TO
HIS NOSE.

> **DUKE V/O**
> Ah, devil ether. It makes you behave
> like the village drunkard in some
> early Irish novel...total loss of all
> basic motor skills: blurred vision,
> no balance, numb tongue —
>> (throws away kleenex)
> The mind recoils in horror, unable to
> communicate with the spinal column.
> Which is interesting, because you can
> actually watch yourself behaving in
> this terrible way, but you can't con-
> trol it.

DUKE and GONZO approach the entrance with elaborate care —
taking one step at a time — trying to keep ahead of the
drug.

> **DUKE V/O**
> You approach the turnstiles and know
> that when you get there, you have to
> give the man two dollars or he won't
> let you inside...but when you get
> there, everything goes wrong.

THE ETHER KICKS IN:

DUKE and GONZO BOUNCE off the walls, CRASH into OLD
LADIES, GIGGLE HELPLESSLY as they try to pay — HANDS
FLAPPING CRAZILY, unable to get money out of their pock-
ets.

> **DUKE V/O**
> Some angry Rotarian shoves you and
> you think: What's happening here?
> What's going on? Then you hear your-
> self mumbling.

> **DUKE**
>> (Mumbling)
> Dogs fucked the Pope, no fault of
> mine. Watch out!... Why money? My

Sc 36

TRACK BACK

name is Brinks; I was born... Born?

> **GONZO**
> Get sheep over side ... women and
> children to armored car ... orders
> from Captain Zeep.

The ATTENDANTS indulgently escort them through the TURN-STILES.

> **DUKE V/O**
> Ether is the perfect drug for Las
> Vegas. In this town they love a
> drunk. Fresh meat. So they put us
> through the turnstiles and turned us
> loose inside.

INT. BAZOOKO CIRCUS CASINO.— NIGHT

Flames shoot up from below the casino. Above, a HIGH WIRE ACT with FOUR MUZZLED WOLVERINES, SIX NYMPHET SISTERS FROM SAN DIEGO, TWO SILVER PAINTED POLACK BROTHERS, and THREE KOREAN KITTENS.

The WOLVERINE chases a NYMPHET through the air. TWO POLACKS swing at it from opposite sides and they are instantly locked in a death battle.

All plummet to the nets suspended over the GAMBLING TABLES and SLOT MACHINES. No one looks up. The GAMBLERS REMAIN INTENT ON THE SPINNING ROULETTE WHEEL, THE TURN OF THE CARD, THE ROLL OF A DICE.

> **DUKE V/O**
> Bazooko Circus is what the whole hep
> world would be doing Saturday night
> if the Nazis had won the war. This
> was the Sixth Reich.

Something causes DUKE to look down. A dwarf carrying drinks on a tray is tugging Duke's pants leg trying to get him to move out of the way.

> **DUKE V/O (CONT'D)**
> A drug person can learn to cope with
> things like seeing their dead grand-
> mother crawling up their leg with a
> knife in her teeth but, nobody should
> be asked to handle this trip.

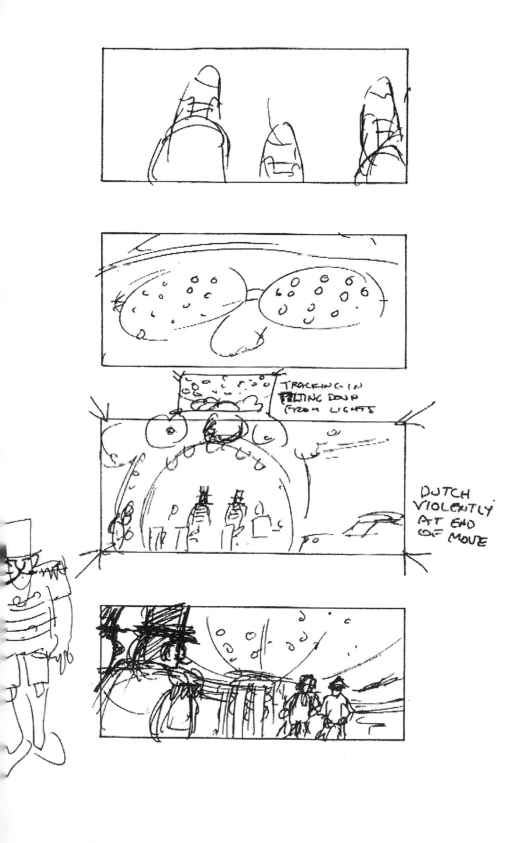

TRACKING IN
TILTING DOWN
FROM LIGHTS

DUTCH
VIOLENTLY
AT END
OF MOVE

GONZO and DUKE go upstairs walking past funhouse booths.
One of them is manned by an orangutan in costume. A FAIR-
GROUND BARKER grabs DUKE.

> **FAIRGROUND BARKER**
> Stand in front of this <u>fantastic</u>
> <u>machine</u>, my friend. For just 99 cents
> your likeness will appear <u>200 hundred</u>
> <u>feet tall</u> on a screen above downtown
> Las Vegas.

On a TV monitor a 200 FOOT HIGH DRUNKARD looms over the
Las Vegas skyline screaming OBSCENITIES.

> **FAIRGROUND BARKER**
> 99 cents more for a voice message.
> Say <u>whatever you want</u>, fella. They'll
> hear you, don't worry about that.
> Remember, <u>you'll be 200 foot tall</u>!

> **ANOTHER BARKER**
> Step right up! Shoot the pasties off
> the nipples of this ten-foot bull-
> dyke and win a cotton candy goat!

INT. BAZOOKO CIRCUS REVOLVING MERRY-GO-ROUND BAR — NIGHT

DUKE and GONZO sit on the revolving platform. GONZO stares
— glassy eyed — coming apart.

> **GONZO**
> I hate to say this, but this place is
> getting to me. I think I'm getting
> <u>The Fear</u>.

> **DUKE**
> Nonsense. We came here to find the
> American Dream, and now we're right
> in the vortex you want to quit. You
> must realize that we've found the
> Main Nerve.

> **GONZO**
> That's what gives me The Fear.

> **DUKE**
> Look over there. Two women fucking a
> Polar Bear.

                    GONZO

Please, don't tell me those things..
Not now.
          (signals the waitress for
              two Wild Turkeys)
This is my last drink. How much money
can you lend me?

                    DUKE

Not much. Why?

                    GONZO

I have to go.

                    DUKE

GO?

                    GONZO

Yes. Leave the country. Tonight.

                    DUKE

Calm down. You'll be straight in a
few hours.

                    GONZO

No. This is serious. One more hour in
this town and I'll kill somebody!

                    DUKE

OK. I'll lend you some money. Let's
go outside and see how much we have
left.

                    GONZO

Can we make it?

                    DUKE

That depends on how many people we
fuck with between here and the door.

                    GONZO

I want to leave fast.

                    DUKE

OK. Lets pay this bill and get up
very slowly. It's going to be a long
walk.
          (signals waitress who
              comes over)

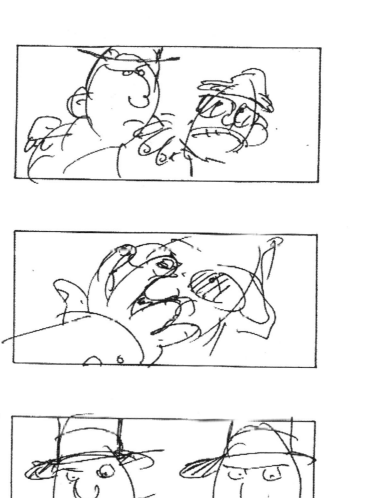

                              GONZO
                    (suddenly to waitress)
              Do they pay you to screw that bear?

                            WAITRESS
          What?

                              DUKE
          He's just kidding.
                          (to GONZO)
          Come on, Doc — lets go downstairs and
          gamble.

GONZO trembles with fear — walks to the edge of the
turntable.

                              GONZO
              When does this thing stop?

                              DUKE
          It won't stop. It's not ever going to
          stop.

DUKE carefully steps off the turntable.

GONZO, eyes staring blindly ahead, squinting in fear and
confusion, rooted to the spot, is carried away.

                              DUKE
              Don't move you'll come around.

DUKE reaches out to grab GONZO, who jumps back — keeps
going around.

The BARTENDER narrows his eyes at them.

DUKE steps onto the merry-go-round — hurries round the bar
— approaching GONZO from the blind side and shoves GONZO
from behind. GONZO goes down with a hellish scream. DUKE
approaches him with his hands in the air. Smiling.

                              DUKE
              You fell. Let's go

GONZO refuses to move and stands tense, fists clenched,
looking for somebody to hit...an old woman perhaps?

                          DUKE (CONT'D)
              OK. You stay here and go to jail. I'm

MOVING
TRAFFIC
IN NIGHT
VIEW OF WINDOW

Sc 39

leaving.

DUKE walks fast towards the stairs. GONZO catches up with
him.

> ### GONZO
> Did you see that? Some sonofabitch
> kicked me in the back.

> ### DUKE
> Probably the bartender. He wanted to
> stomp you for what you said to the
> waitress.

> ### GONZO
> Good God! Let's get out of here!
> Where's the elevator?

> ### DUKE
> (turning him in the opposite
> direction)
> Don't go near that elevator. That's
> just what they want us to do ... trap
> us in a steel box and take us down to
> the basement.

EXT. BAZOOKO CIRCUS CASINO — NIGHT

DUKE and GONZO stumble out of the entrance.

> ### DUKE
> Don't run. They'd like any excuse to
> shoot us.

> ### GONZO
> (in an exteneded fall)
> You drive! I think there's something
> wrong with me.

INT. MINT HOTEL CORRIDOR OUTSIDE THEIR SUITE — NIGHT

DUKE AND GONZO RUN MADLY DOWN THE CORRIDOR ... DUKE TAK-
ING CARE NOT TO STEP ON THE PATTERNED PART OF THE CARPET.

GONZO STRUGGLES with the key in the lock.

> ### GONZO
> Those bastards have <u>changed the loc</u>k
> on us. They probably <u>searched the</u>

<u>room</u>. Jesus, we're finished!

The door SUDDENLY SWINGS OPEN. DUKE and GONZO fall inside.

INT. MINT HOTEL SUITE — NIGHT

>   GONZO
>   Bolt everything! Use all chains!

DUKE locks the door. The suite is crowded with ROOM SER-
VICE GOODIES. DUKE turns to see GONZO staring at <u>two</u>
hotel room keys. EVERYTHING STOPS.

>   GONZO
>   Where did this one come from?

DUKE snatches a key.

>   DUKE
>   That's Lacerda's room.

GONZO smiles a slow smile....

>   GONZO
>   Yeah ... I thought we might need
>   it....

>   DUKE
>   What for?

GONZO snatches the key back.

>   GONZO
>   Let's go up there and blast him out
>   of bed with the fire hose.

>   DUKE
>   No, we should leave the poor bastard
>   alone. I get the feeling that he's
>   avoiding us for some reason.

>   GONZO
>   Don't kid yourself. That Portuguese
>   son of a bitch is <u>dangerous</u>. He's
>   watching us like a hawk.

>   DUKE
>   He told me he was turning in early...

GONZO utters an anguished cry — slaps the wall with both hands.

                    GONZO
          That dirty bastard! I knew it! He's
          got hold of my woman!

                    DUKE
                 (laughing)
          That little blonde groupie with the
          film crew? You think he sodomized
          her?

                    GONZO
          That's right, laugh about it! You
          goddamn honkies are all the same!

GONZO SLASHES A GRAPEFRUIT with a HUGE RAZOR SHARP HUNTING KNIFE. DUKE blanches.

                    DUKE
          Where'd you get that knife?

GONZO SLICES THE GRAPEFRUIT — MANIACAL.

                    GONZO
          Room service sent it up. I wanted
          something to cut the limes.

GONZO SLICES THE GRAPEFRUIT — INTO EIGHTHS!

                    DUKE
          What limes?

GONZO SLICES — SIXTEENTHS!

                    GONZO
          They didn't have any. They don't grow
          in the desert.

SLICE! SLICE! SLICE!

                    GONZO
          That dirty toad bastard! I knew I
          should have taken him out when I had
          the chance. Now he has her.

SLICE! SLICE! SLICE! GONZO SLASHES INSANELY!

DUKE watches — straight-faced.

> ### DUKE V/O
> I remember the girl. We'd had a prob-
> lem with her in the elevator a few
> hours earlier: my attorney had made a
> fool of himself.

INT. ELEVATOR DAY (FLASHBACK)

An elevator door opens to reveal the SMILING FACES OF
LACERDA, THE BLONDE TV REPORTER AND HER CREW.

DUKE and GONZO stagger in.

LACERDA drops his smile. He's standing beside the BLONDE
TV REPORTER. A trembling GONZO moonily turns his eyes onto
her.

> ### BLONDE TV REPORTER
> (to Gonzo)
> You must be a rider. What class are
> you in?

> ### GONZO
> Class? What the fuck do you mean?

> ### BLONDE TV REPORTER
> What do you ride? We're filming the
> race for a TV series — maybe we can
> use you

> ### GONZO
> Use me?

> ### DUKE V/O
> Mother of God, I thought. Here it
> comes.

GONZO is TREMBLING BADLY. There's a moment of uncomfort-
able silence.

> ### GONZO
> (suddenly shouting)
> I ride the BIG ONES! The really BIG
> fuckers!

GONZO shows his teeth to LACERDA. DUKE laughs trying to
defuse the scene.

                          DUKE
          The Vincent Black Shadow. We're with
          the Factory Team.

                       TV CAMERMAN
          Bullshit.

GONZO stills — becomes dangerous — zeros in on the TV
CAMERAMAN — groin to groin ...

                          GONZO
          Wait a minute, pardon me lady, but I
          think there's some kind of ignorant
          chicken-sucker in this car who needs
          his face cut open. You cheap honky
          faggots! Which one of you wants to
          get cut?!

DEAD SILENCE.

Ding! The elevator door opens, but nobody moves. The door
closes.

Next floor. Ding! The door opens again. A middle-aged couple start to get in. Change their minds. The door closes.

INT CORRIDOR — DAY

DUKE and GONZO run down the corridor. GONZO LAUGHS WILDLY.

                          GONZO
          Spooked! They were spooked! Like rats
          in a death cage!

INT. MINT HOTEL SUITE — DAY

DUKE and GONZO CRASH into their hotel suite — BOLT THE
DOOR. GONZO stops laughing.

                          GONZO
          Goddamn. It's serious now. That girl
          understood. She fell in love with me.

END FLASHBACK.

INT. MINT HOTEL SUITE — NIGHT

SLICE! SLICE! SLICE! GONZO with the BIG HUNTING KNIFE —
sliced grapefruit segments everywhere.

GONZO

Let's go up there and castrate that
fucker!

GONZO pauses — A MAD THOUGHT — turns to DUKE.

GONZO
(squinting suspiciously)
Have you made a deal with him?
Did you put him on to her?

DUKE
(backing slowly towards
the door)
Look you better put that blade away
and get your head straight. I have to
put the car in the lot.

DUKE V/O

One of the things you learn, after
years of dealing with drug people, is
that you can turn your back on a person, but never turn your back on a
drug. Especially when it's waving a

razor-sharp hunting knife in your
eyes.

INT CASINO/LOBBY MINT HOTEL

The MAGAZINE REPORTER is on the telephone.

> **MAGAZINE REPORTER**
> Las Vegas at dawn. The racers are
> still asleep, the dust is still on
> the desert, fifty thousand dollars in
> prize money, slumbers darkly in the
> office safe at Del Webb's fabulous
> Mint Hotel ...

DUKE walks past the REPORTER — into THE CASINO, THE SAD,
MEAGRE CROWDS AROUND THE CRAP TABLES. No joy. DUKE
watches.

> **DUKE V/O**
> Who are these people? These faces!
> Where do they come from? They look
> like caricatures of used car dealers
> from Dallas. And, sweet Jesus, there
> are a hell of a lot of them at four-

DETAILS
OF GAMBLERS

MEDIC
CHECKING
DEAD
GAMBLER

BAR

Little
Old lady
2t Great
SHOT

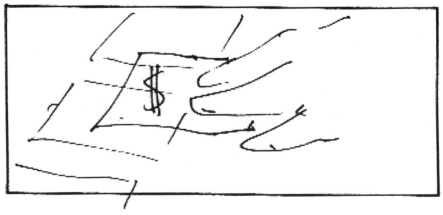

> thirty on a Monday morning. Still
> humping the American dream, that
> vision of the big winner somehow
> emerging from the last minute pre-
> dawn chaos of a stale Vegas casino.

DUKE stops at the Money Wheel, puts down a two dollar
bill on a number, the wheel turns, he loses.

                         DUKE
        You bastards!

                       DUKE V/O
        No. Calm down. Learn to ENJOY losing.

INT. MINT HOTEL SUITE. — NIGHT

DUKE walks back into the room. We hear the LOUD STRAINS
OF THREE DOG NIGHT'S "JOY TO THE WORLD."

He walks to the bathroom and opens the door.

INT. MINT HOTEL SUITE BATHROOM — NIGHT

Submerged in green water, GONZO WALLOWS in the steaming
tub. Soap labels and grapefruit rinds float on the sur-
face. A large empty pack of Neutrogena soap lies on the
floor. The shower is on - the tub overflowing. THE TAPE
RECORDER PLAYS, from where it's plugged into the razor
socket over the sink.

DUKE turns off the shower — notices a HUGE HUNK OF CHEWED
UP WHITE BLOTTER.

                         DUKE
        You ate ALL THIS ACID?

No answer.

                         DUKE
              (turning down the volume)
        You evil son of a bitch. You better
        hope there's some Thorazine in that
        bag, because if there's not, you're
        in bad trouble.

                        GONZO
        Music! Turn it up. Put that tape on.

95

                    DUKE

What tape?

                    GONZO

Jefferson Airplane. "White Rabbit." I
want a rising sound.

                    DUKE

You're doomed. I'm leaving here in
two hours and then they're going to
come up here and beat the mortal shit
out of you with big saps. Right there
in that tub.

                    GONZO

I dig my own graves. Green water and
the White Rabbit. Put it on.

                    DUKE

OK. But do me one last favor, will
you. Can you give me two hours?
That's all I ask — just two hours to
sleep before tomorrow. I suspect it's
going to be a very difficult day.

He switches on the tape. "WHITE RABBIT" begins to build.

                    GONZO
                    (coolly)
Of course, I'm your attorney, I'll
give you all the time you need, at my
normal rates: $45 an hour — but
you'll be wanting a cushion, so, why
don't you just lay one of those $100
bills down there beside the radio,
and fuck off?

                    DUKE

How about a check?

                    GONZO

Whatever's right.

DUKE moves the radio as far from the tub as he can and
leaves, closing the door behind him.

INT. MINT HOTEL SUITE — NIGHT

DUKE goes across to the sofa and crashes —

                        96

exhausted.Suddenly a great ripping and crashing noise in
the bathroom.

> GONZO V/O
> Help! You bastard! I need help!

DUKE JUMPS up — crosses to the bathroom door, muttering.

> DUKE
> Shit, he's killing himself!

INT. BATHROOM — NIGHT

DUKE RUSHES IN. GONZO flails — trying to reach the radio
with the shower curtain pole which he has ripped from its
mounts.

> GONZO
> (snarling)
> I want that fucking radio!

DUKE GRABS THE RADIO.

> DUKE
> Don't touch it! Get back in that tub!

> GONZO
> Back the tape up. I need it again!
> Let it roll! Just as high as the
> fucker can go! And when it comes to
> that fantastic note where the rabbit
> bites its own head off, I want you to
> THROW THAT FUCKING RADIO INTO THE TUB
> WITH ME!

DUKE stares down at GONZO.

> DUKE
> Not me. It would blast you through
> the wall — stone dead in ten seconds
> and they'd make me explain it!

> GONZO
> BULLSHIT! Don't make me use this.

HIS ARM LASHES OUT OF THE WATER, HOLDING THE KNIFE.

> DUKE
> Jesus.

                                GONZO
                    Do it! I want to get HIGHER!

DUKE considers this. He's had enough.

                                DUKE
                    Okay. You're right. This is probably
                    the only solution.
                            (holds the PLUGGED IN
                            TAPE/RADIO over the tub)
                    Let me make sure I have it all lined
                    up. You want me to throw this thing
                    into the tub when "WHITE RABBIT"
                    peaks. Is that it?

GONZO falls back into the water, smiling gratefully.

                                GONZO
                    Fuck yes. I was beginning to think I
                    was going to have to go out and get
                    one of the goddamn maids to do it.

                                DUKE
                    Are you ready?

He switches "WHITE RABBIT" back on. GONZO HOWLS AND MOANS
AND THRASHES TO THE MUSIC, straining to get over the top.

Meanwhile, DUKE picks up a grapefruit from the sink — a
good two-pounder, he gets a grip on it... and when "WHITE
RABBIT" peaks... HE HURLS IT INTO THE TUB LIKE A CANNON-
BALL.

GONZO SCREAMS CRAZILY, THRASHING AND CHURNING — CAUSING A
TIDAL WAVE.

DUKE JERKS THE RADIO CABLE OUT OF THE SOCKET — SLAMS OUT
OF THE BATHROOM.

INT. MINT HOTEL SUITE. — NIGHT

DUKE slumps onto the sofa.

SILENCE.

GONZO RIPS OPEN THE BATHROOM DOOR, his eyes unfocused. HE
WAVES THE RAZOR SHARP BLADE out in front of him — LUNGES
at DUKE. DUKE WHIPS OUT A CAN OF MACE.

                              DUKE
              MACE! YOU WANT THIS?

GONZO stops — hisses.

                              GONZO

           You bastard! You'd do that, wouldn't
           you?

                              DUKE
                          (laughs)
           Why worry? You'll like it. Nothing in
           the world like a Mace high. Forty-
           five minutes on your knees with the
           dry heaves ..

                              GONZO

           You cheap honky sonofabitch ...

                              DUKE

           Why not? Hell, just a minute ago, you
           were asking me to <u>kill</u> you! And now
           you want to kill <u>me</u>! What I should
           do, goddamnit, is call the <u>police</u>!

                              GONZO

           The cops?

                              DUKE

           There's no choice. I wouldn't dare go
           to sleep with you wandering around
           with a head full of acid and wanting
           to slice me up with that goddamn
           knife!

                              GONZO
                          (mumbles)
           Who said anything about slicing you
           up? I just wanted to carve a little Z
           on your forehead. Nothing serious.

GONZO shrugs and reaches for a cigarette on top of the TV
set.

                              DUKE
                    (menaces him with the MACE)
           Get back in that tub. Eat some reds
           and try to calm down. Smoke some
           grass, shoot some smack — shit, do

                              99

                    whatever you have to do, but let me
                    get some rest.

GONZO turns toward the bathroom — suddenly sad.

                              GONZO
                    Hell, yes. You really need some
                    sleep. You have to work. Goddamn.
                    What a bummer. Try to rest. Don't let
                    me keep you up.

GONZO shuffles back into the bathroom. DUKE wedges a chair
up against the bathroom doorknob and puts the mace can
next to the clock.

DUKE turns on the TV. WHITE NOISE FILLS THE ROOM. He col-
lapses onto the sofa and lights ups his lightbulb has
pipe.

                            DUKE V/O
                    Ignore the nightmare in the bathroom.
                    Just another ugly refugee from the
                    Love Generation.

The WHITE NOISE snow storm on the TV is reflected in his
face. The camera pulls back revealing THE ENTIRE WALL
BEHIND HIM TO BE SWIRLING WITH THE FIZZING SNOWSTORM PAT-
TERN.

                            DUKE V/O
                    My attorney had never been able to
                    accept the notion — often espoused by
                    former drug abusers — that you can
                    get a lot higher without drugs than
                    with them.
                    And neither have I, for that matter.

The pattern on the wall changes to A 60'S VISCOUS OIL
LIGHTSHOW PATTERN. With DUKE still sitting in the fore-
ground, the projected image widens to reveal the interior
of A HAIGHT ASHBURY DANCE HALL full of DANCING PROTO-HIP-
PIES.

INT. MATRIX CLUB — NIGHT.

A slightly YOUNGER DUKE moves through the throng. All the
action is in a DREAMLIKE SLOW-MOTION.

                              100

MAKE BATHROOM DOOR
SHORT SO LIGHT CAN
FLOOD OUT

TEST

COUCH
BEGINS
TO FLOAT

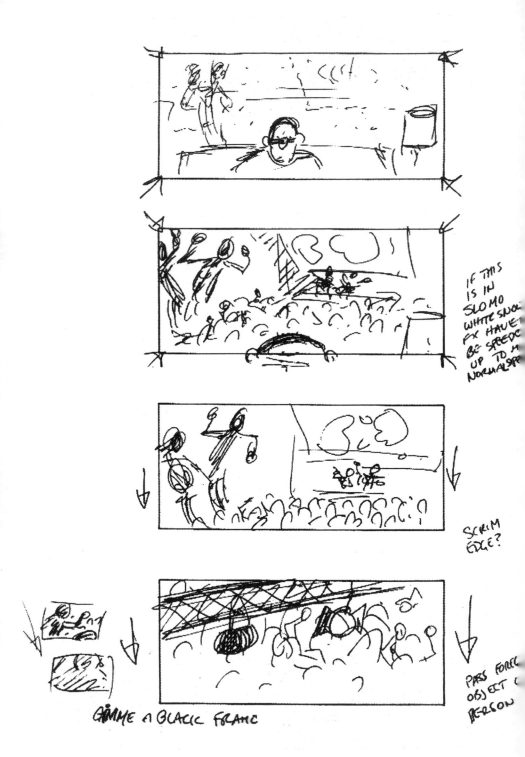

IF THIS
IS IN
SLO MO
WHITE SNO
FX HAVE
BE SPEED
UP TO N
NORMAL SP

SCRIM
EDGE?

GIMME A BLACK FRAME

PASS FORE
OBJECT (
PERSON

YOUNGER
DUKE

WHITE SNOW DISSOLVE
PULL BACK TO SEE IMAGE ON TV

                    DUKE V/O
        I recall one night in the Matrix.
        There I was — a victim of the Drug
        Explosion. A natural street freak,
        just eating whatever came by.

A ROAD-PERSON with a big pack on his back is shouting.
The sound of his voice, like his movements, is in slow-
motion.

                    ROAD-PERSON
        Anybody want some L ... S ... D ...?
        I got all the makin's right here. All
        I need is a place to cook.

The camera pushes right into the ROAD-PERSON's mouth.

INT. MATRIX MEN'S ROOM — NIGHT

Still in slow motion, the YOUNGER DUKE is trying to eat a
HUGE SPANSULE OF ACID. With difficulty.

                    DUKE V/O
        I decided to eat only <u>half</u> at first.
        Good thinking. But I spilled the rest
        on the sleeve of my red Pendleton
        shirt.

DUKE stares at his sleeve, uncertain what to do. C/U of
the door to the men's room as a MUSICIAN enters speaking
in slow-motion.

                    MUSICIAN
        What's the trouble?

                    DUKE
              (also in slow-motion)
        Well, all this white stuff on my
        sleeve is LSD.

The MUSICIAN approaches and looks down at DUKE'S arm. A
long pause.

Cut back to tight shot of door as it opens and a very
clean-cut, PREPPY, STOCKBROKER TYPE enters. He freezes in
horror. We cut to his POV. DUKE is standing in the middle
of the men's room with the MUSICIAN hunkered down at his
side ... sucking on his sleeve. A very gross tableau. The
STOCKBROKER slowly eases out of the room.

> ### DUKE V/O
> With a bit of luck his life was
> ruined — forever thinking that just
> behind some narrow door in all his
> favorite bars, men in red Pendleton
> shirts are getting incredible kicks
> from things he'll never know.

INT. A BAR — YEARS LATER — NIGHT.

The STOCKBROKER LOOKING CONSIDERABLY OLDER sits looking
lost, confused, a nervous wreck. The image flares out in
a TV white noise snowstorm.

INT. MINT HOTEL SUITE — NIGHT

DUKE sits staring at the TV.

> ### DUKE V/O
> Strange memories on this nervous
> night in Las Vegas.
> > (he gets up, pours
> > himself a drink)
> Has it been five years? Six? It seems
> like a lifetime — the kind of peak
> that never comes again. San Francisco
> in the middle sixties was a very spe-
> cial time and place to be a part of.
> But no explanation, no mix of words
> or music or memories can touch that
> sense of knowing that you were there
> and alive in that corner of time and
> the world. Whatever it meant.

DUKE throws open the curtains. Light streams in.

EXT. 1965 STOCK FOOTAGE.

We are in SAN FRANCISCO. IMAGES OF THE TIME FLOOD IN.

> ### DUKE V/O
> THERE WAS MADNESS IN ANY DIRECTION,
> AT ANY HOUR... YOU COULD STRIKE
> SPARKS ANYWHERE. THERE WAS A FANTAS-
> TIC UNIVERSAL SENSE THAT WHATEVER WE
> WERE DOING WAS RIGHT, THAT WE WERE
> WINNING. AND THAT, I THINK, WAS THE
> HANDLE — THAT SENSE OF INEVITABLE
> VICTORY OVER THE FORCES OF OLD AND

BLUE SCREE

IMAGES.

DOCK PLOATT / PROJECTED IMAGES IN ROOM

EVIL. NOT IN ANY MEAN OR MILITARY
SENSE; WE DIDN'T NEED THAT. OUR ENER-
GY WOULD SIMPLY prevail. We had all
the momentum; we were riding the
crest of a high and beautiful wave...

DUKE'S FACE IS SUFFUSED WITH A SADNESS AND SERENITY WE
HAVE NEVER SEEN BEFORE.

>   **DUKE V/O**
> So now, less than five years later,
> you can go up on a steep hill in Las
> Vegas and look west, and with the
> right kind of eyes you can almost see
> the high water mark — that place
> where the wave finally broke and
> rolled back.

The memories dissolve into the night skyline of Vegas.
Suddenly towering over the casinos is a 200 foot high
Nazi shouting "WOODSTOCK ÜBER ALLES!"

INT. MINT HOTEL SUITE — NIGHT

DUKE closes the curtain. The room is in darkness again.

INT. MINT HOTEL SUITE — DAWN

A harsh door buzzer. DUKE jerks awake. Alone. Looking like
shit. Around him is the wreckage of their stay.

>   **DUKE V/O**
> The decision to flee came suddenly.
> Or maybe not.

DUKE opens the door to a BELL BOY with a trolley load of
fruit, drinks and flowers ... and a smile.

>   **BELL BOY**
> Room service!

The BELL BOY wheels the trolley across the room — already
stacked with EVEN MORE BOXES OF GOODIES.

>   **DUKE V/O**
> Maybe I'd planned it all along — sub-
> consciously waiting for the right
> moment. The bill was a factor, I

think. Because I had no money to pay
for it.

DUKE slams the door — starts FRANTICALLY PACKING.

                    DUKE V/O
Our room service tabs had been running somewhere between $29 and $36
per hour, for forty-eight consecutive
hours. Incredible. How could it hap-
pen?

DUKE sees the DISCARDED WRAPPING OF EXPENSIVE, HAND TOOLED
LUGGAGE. A sudden thought. He rushes to GONZO's room —
empty. His plastic briefcase remains on the bed...

                    DUKE V/O
But by the time I asked this ques-
tion, there was no one around to
answer.

DUKE opens the briefcase — finds the .357 MAGNUM inside.

                    DUKE V/O
My attorney was gone. He must have
sensed trouble.

QUICK CUT TO:

EXT. LAS VEGAS AIRPORT — DAY

GONZO WAVES GOODBYE as he boards an airplane with a set
of brand-new fine cowhide luggage.

                    DUKE V/O
        Panic.

INT. CORRIDOR OUTSIDE HOTEL SUITE — DAY

DUKE emerges with his bag and Gonzo's plastic briefcase —
leaves the DO NOT DISTURB sign on the door — checks both
ways, then hurries away down the corridor.

                    DUKE V/O
It crept up my spine like first rising vibes of an acid frenzy. All
these horrible realities began to
dawn on me.

INT. MINT HOTEL ELEVATOR — DAY

An anxiety ridden DUKE watches the floor numbers as the elevator descends. He searches his pockets....

> **DUKE V/O**
> Here I was, alone in Las Vegas, with this goddamned incredibly expensive car, completely twisted on drugs, no cash, no story for the magazine. And on top of everything else I had a gigantic goddamn hotel bill to deal with.

DUKE finds a last crumpled $5 bill.

The door opens. A SECURITY GUARD enters with an OLD LADY IN HANDCUFFS.

DUKE hides the bill — crams back into the corner. Doors close.

> **DUKE V/O**
> I didn't even know who had won the race. Maybe nobody.

INT. MINT HOTEL LOBBY — DAY

DUKE hurries out of the elevator — eyes on a hovering MANAGER. Past the curious look of the reception CLERK.

> **DUKE**
> (muttering to himself)
> How would Horatio Alger have handled this situation?

EXT. MINT HOTEL — DAY

Motoring, DUKE gives his $5 bill to the HOTEL FRONT DOOR-MAN with a smile. The DOORMAN blows a frantic whistle and waves at the CAR BOY.

> **DUKE V/O**
> Stay calm. Stay calm. I'm a relative-ly respectable citizen — a multiple felon, perhaps, but certainly not dangerous.

The CAR BOY pulls up with a screech. DUKE jumps in. The

back seat is stacked with bars of Neutrogena, piles of
Mint 400 T-shirts, boxes of grapefruit.

> **DUKE V/O (CONT'D)**
> Luckily, I had taken the soap and
> grapefruit and other luggage out to
> the car a few hours earlier. Now it
> was only a matter of slipping the
> noose...

DUKE shifts into drive. Deliverance!

> **CLERK'S VOICE**
> MR. DUKE!

DUKE freezes.

> **CLERK'S VOICE**
> Mr. Duke! We've been looking for you!

> **DUKE V/O**
> The game was up. They had me.

> **DUKE**
> (to himself)
> Well, why not? Many fine books have
> been written in prison.

Resigned, DUKE turns off the ignition. A young CLERK
arrives breathlessly with a smile and a YELLOW LETTER IN
HIS HAND.

> **CLERK**
> Sir?
> (thrusts out a TELEGRAM)
> This telegram came for you. Actually,
> it isn't for you. It's for somebody
> named Thompson, but it says 'care of
> Raoul Duke'. Does that make sense?

> **DUKE**
> (barely able to speak)
> Yes ... It makes sense.

DUKE stuffs the telegram into his top pocket.

The CLERK peers into the car — sees part of the enormous
stash inside.

CLERK

I checked the register for this man
Thompson. We don't show him but I
figured he might be part of your
team.

DUKE

He is. Don't worry, I'll get it to
him.

He fires up the engine — eases the RED SHARK into low
gear.

SECURITY GUARDS are looking across — sharing a quiet word
or two.

CLERK

What confused us was Dr. Gonzo's sig-
nature on the telegram from Los
Angeles. When we knew he was right
here in the hotel.

DUKE

You did the right thing. Never try to
understand a press message. About
half the time we use codes — especially with Dr. Gonzo.

CLERK

Tell me. When will the doctor be
awake?

DUKE
(tenses)
Awake? What do you mean?

DUKE's eyes are on the SECURITY GUARDS — moving closer.

CLERK
(uncomfortably)
Well...the manager, Mr. Heem, would
like to meet him. Nothing unusual.
Mr. Heem likes to meet all our large
accounts... put them on a personal
basis... just a chat and a handshake,
you understand.

DUKE

Of course. But if I were you, I'd

leave the Doctor alone until after
he's eaten breakfast. He's a very
crude man.

DUKE edges the car forward, but is stopped by the CLERK.

                    CLERK
But he will be available? Perhaps
later this morning?

                    DUKE
Look. That telegram was all scram-
bled. It was actually from Thompson,
not to him. Western Union must have
gotten the names reversed. I have to
get going. I have to get out to the
track.

                    CLERK
There's no hurry! The race is over!

                    DUKE
              (taking off)
Not for me.

He waves the CLERK off the car — roars away.

                    CLERK
Let's have lunch!

                    DUKE
Righto!

DUST BLOWING
EARTH
MOVING
EQUIPMENT
~ BKGND.

WELCOME
TO
LOS VEGAS

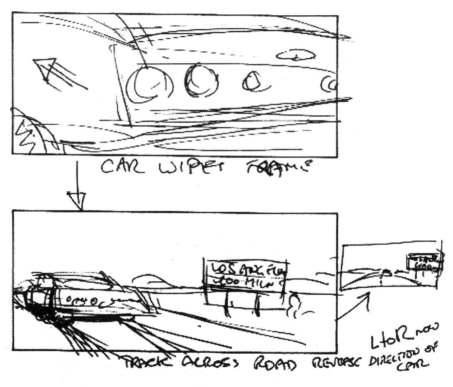

CAR WIPER FRAME?

TRACK ACROSS ROAD REVERSE DIRECTION OF CAR

L to R now

EXT. ROAD OUT OF VEGAS — DAY

DUKE drives the RED SHARK out of Vegas.

A "YOU ARE LEAVING LAS VEGAS" sign flashes past.

Bob Dylan plays: 'Memphis Blues Again — *"Aaww, Mama, can this really be the end...?"*

A sign: LOS ANGELES — 400 miles.

DUKE V/O
Jesus, bad waves of paranoia, madness, fear and loathing — intolerable

vibrations in this place. Get out!
The weasels were closing in. I could
smell the ugly brutes. Flee!

DUKE drives fast.

>   **DUKE**
> Do me one last favor Lord: just give
> me five more high-speed hours before
> you bring the hammer down; just let
> me get rid of this goddamn car and
> off of this horrible desert.

A sign flashes "YOU CAN RUN BUT YOU CAN'T HIDE."

A patrol car pulls out behind him, lights flashing.

>   **DUKE (CONT'D)**
> You evil bastard! This is your work!
> You'd better take care of me, Lord...
> because if you don't you're going to
> have me on your hands.

The patrol car screams after the RED SHARK.

>   **DUKE V/O**
> Few people understand the psychology
> of dealing with a Highway Traffic
> Cop. Your normal speeder will panic
> and immediately pull over to the
> side. This is wrong.

DUKE floors the gas pedal.

>   **DUKE V/O**
> It arouses contempt in the cop heart.

THE SPEEDOMETER CLIMBS STEADILY.

DUKE V/O

Make the bastard chase you. He will
follow. But he won't know what to
make of your blinker signal that says
you're about to turn right.

DUKE signals right. The RED SHARK screams at 120 mph.

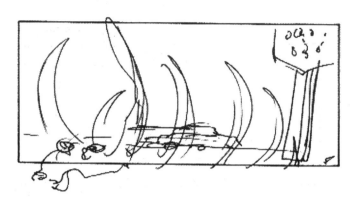

SERIES OF DISTRESSING DEATH SIGNS

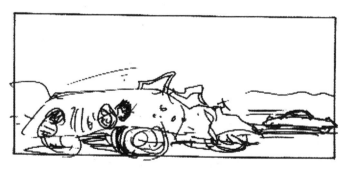

116

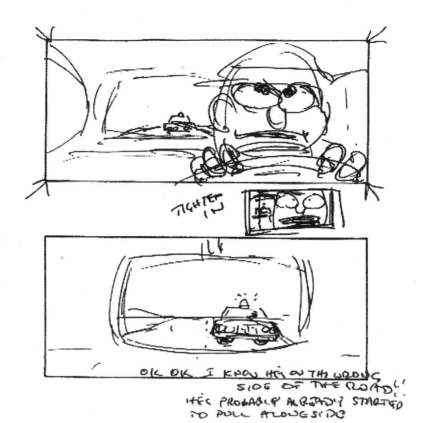

TIGHTER
IN

OK OK. I KNOW HE'S ON THE WRONG
SIDE OF THE ROAD!!
HE'S PROBABLY ALREADY STARTED
TO PULL ALONGSIDE

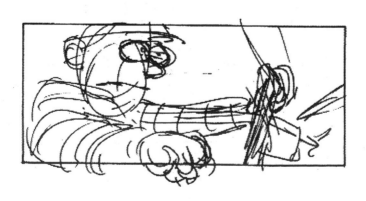

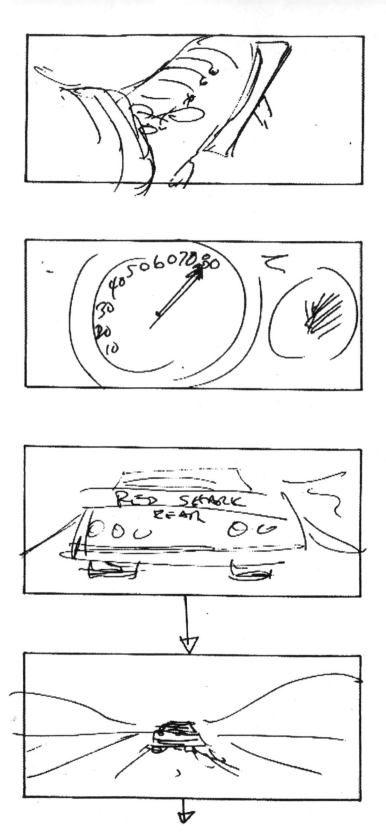

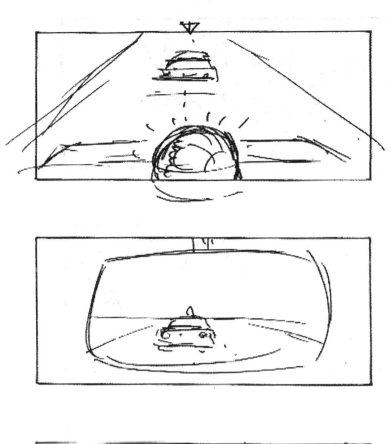

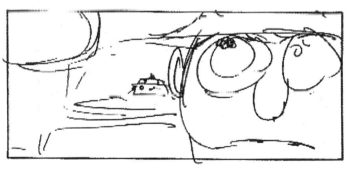

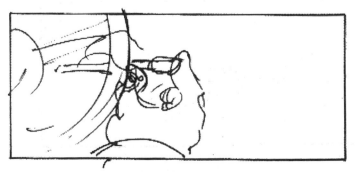

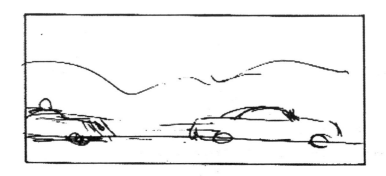

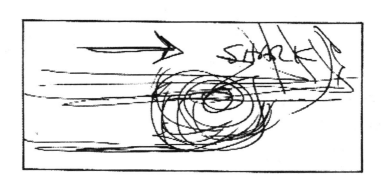

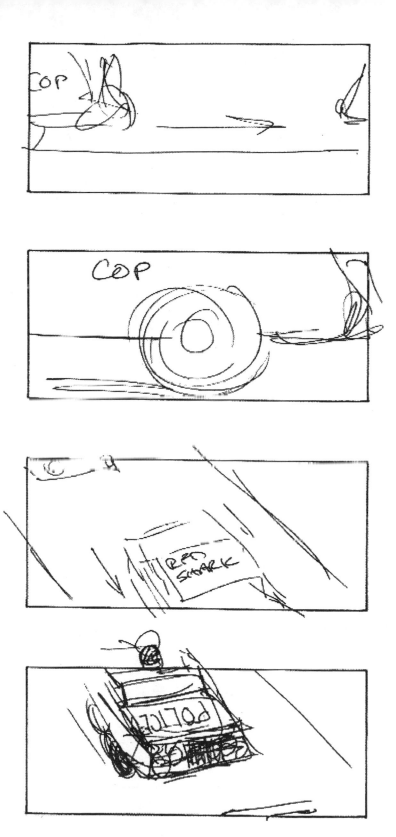

SPLIT DIOPTER

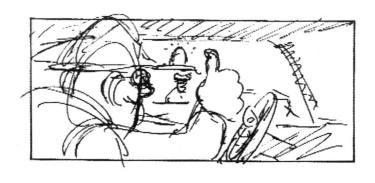

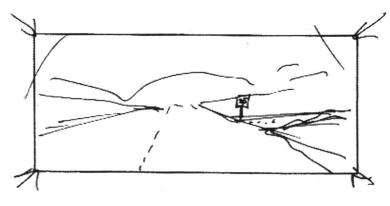

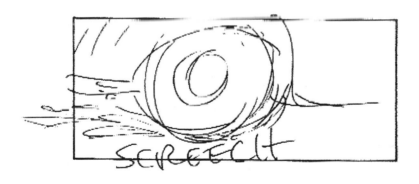

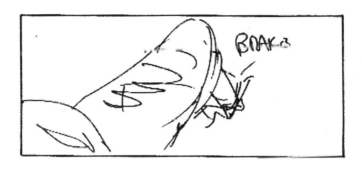

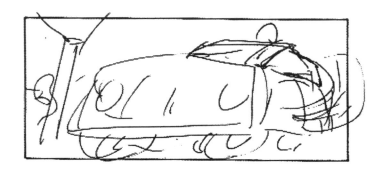

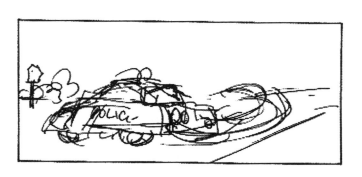

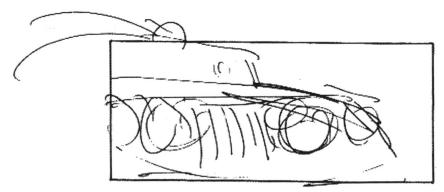

DUKE V/O
          This is to let him know you're look-
          ing for a proper place to pull off
          and talk.

AN EXIT OFF RAMP: MAX SPEED 25.

DUKE hits the brakes. The COP brakes.

                    DUKE V/O
          It will take him a moment to realize
          that he is about to make 180 degree
          turn at speed ... but you will be
          ready for it, braced for the G's and
          the fast heel toe work.

The patrol car spins and fishtails crazily out of control.

EXT. SCENIC PICNIC AREA — DAY

The patrol car comes skidding around the corner. DUKE
stands beside the RED SHARK, completely relaxed and smiling.

The HIGHWAY PATROLMAN gets out of the car, screaming.

                    HIGHWAY PATROLMAN
          Just what the FUCK did you think you
          were doing?!

DUKE smiles.

                    HIGHWAY PATROLMAN
          May I see your license.

                    DUKE
          Of course, officer.

DUKE reaches for it. And BOTH MEN look down at a beer can
— which DUKE had, somehow, forgotten was in his hand.

                    DUKE V/O
          I knew I was fucked.

The COP relaxes — actually smiles ... He reaches out for
DUKE'S wallet, then holds out his other hand for the
beer.

                    HIGHWAY PATROLMAN
          Could I have that, please?

                         125

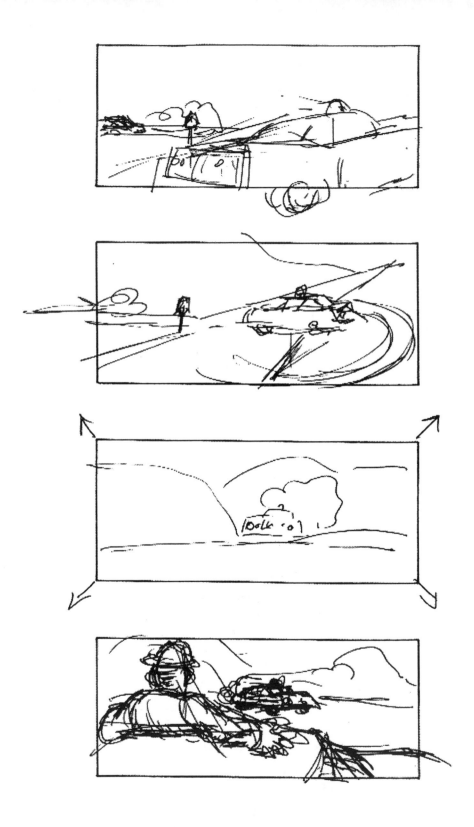

                              DUKE
              Why not? It was getting warm anyway.

The HIGHWAY PATROLMAN takes it, pours out the beer —
glances in the back seat of the RED SHARK. Amongst the
bars of soap...A case of warm beer. DUKE smiles back at
him.

                        HIGHWAY PATROLMAN
              You realize ...

                              DUKE
              Yeah. I know. I'm guilty. I under-
              stand that. I knew it was a crime but
              I did it anyway. Shit, why argue? I'm
              a fucking criminal.

                        HIGHWAY PATROLMAN
              That's a strange attitude.

He looks at DUKE thoughtfully.

                        HIGHWAY PATROLMAN
              You know — I get the feeling you
              could use a nap. There's a rest area
              up ahead. Why don't you pull over and
              sleep a few hours?

                              DUKE
              A nap won't help. I've been awake for
              too long — three or four nights. I
              can't even remember. If I go to sleep
              now, I'm dead for twenty hours.

The HIGHWAY PATROLMAN smiles.

                        HIGHWAY PATROLMAN
              Okay. Here's how it is. What goes
              into my book, as of noon, is that I
              apprehended you ... for driving too
              fast, and advised you to proceed no
              further than the next rest area ...
              your stated destination, right? Where
              you plan to take a long nap. Do I
              make myself clear?

                              DUKE
              How far is Baker? I was hoping to
              stop there for lunch.

                              127

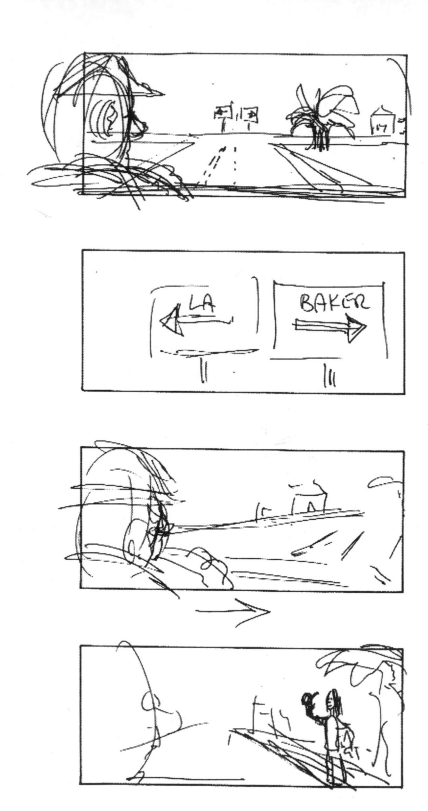

ALMOST TO CAMERA

ALMOST TO CAMERA

BETTER FRAME

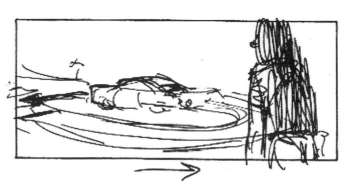

HIGHWAY PATROLMAN
Not my jurisdiction. The city limits
are two point two miles beyond the
rest area. Can you make it that far?

DUKE
I'll try. I've been wanting to go to
Baker for a long time. I've heard a
lot about it.

The PATROLMAN holds the door for DUKE who gets in.

HIGHWAY PATROLMAN
Excellent seafood. With a mind like
yours, you'll probably want to try
the land-crab. Try the Majestic
Diner.

The PATROLMAN slams the door shut.

EXT. DESERT ROAD — DAY

DUKE drives away — teeth gritted.

DUKE V/O
I felt raped. The Pig had done me on
all fronts, and now he was going off
to chuckle about it — on the west
side of town, waiting for me to make
a run for L.A.

DUKE drives past the rest area to an intersection where
he signals to turn right into Baker. As the approaches
the turn he sees the HITCHHIKER! As DUKE slows to make
the turn their eyes meet. DUKE is about to wave — but the
HITCHHIKER drops his thumb.

DUKE
Great Jesus, it's him.

Sc 65

"I FELT RAPED. -"

DUKE, spooked, SPINS THE RED SHARK round — ROARS BACK THE
WAY HE CAME.

EXT. BAKER TRUCK STOP — DAY

DUKE on the public phone booth — screaming.

> ### DUKE
> They've nailed me! I'm trapped in
> some stinking desert crossroads
> called Baker. I don't have much time.

Se66

MAYBE BOOTH IS TIPPED

The fuckers are closing in. They'll
hunt me down like a beast!

INT. GONZO'S OFFICE — DAY

GONZO sits surrounded by legal papers and law books.
Mexican Day of the Dead masks hang from the walls —
flame-red demons.

GONZO
Who? You sound a little paranoid.

EXT. BAKER TRUCK STOP — DAY

DUKE screams — sweat pouring.

DUKE
You bastard! I need a lawyer immediately!

INT. GONZO'S OFFICE — DAY

> GONZO
>
> What are you doing in Baker? Didn't
> you get my telegram?

EXT. BAKER TRUCK STOP — DAY

> DUKE
>
> What? Fuck telegrams. I'm in trouble.
> You worthless bastard. I'll cripple
> your ass for this! All that shit in
> the car is yours! You understand
> that? When I finish testifying out
> here you'll be disbarred!

INT. GONZO'S OFFICE — DAY

> GONZO
>
> You're supposed to be in Vegas. We
> have a suite at the Flamingo. I was
> just about to leave for the airport.

EXT. BAKER TRUCK STOP — DAY

DUKE pulls out the telegram from his top pocket.

> GONZO'S VOICE
>
> You brainless scumbag! You're sup-
> posed to be covering the National
> District Attorney's conference! I
> made all the reservations ... rented
> a white Cadillac convertible ... the
> whole thing is arranged! What the
> hell are you doing out there in the
> middle of the fucking desert?

DUKE stares at the telegram.

> DUKE
>
> Never mind. It's all a big joke. I'm
> actually sitting beside the pool at
> the Flamingo. I'm talking from a
> portable phone. Some dwarf brought it
> out from the casino. I have total
> credit! Can you grasp that?
>   (shouts)
> Don't come anywhere near this place!
> Foreigners aren't welcome here!

DUKE, breathing heavily, hangs up phone.

EXT. DESERT — DAY

C/U of .357 Magnum cylinder being spun.

> **DUKE V/O**
> Well. This is how the world works.

C/U An IGUANA basks in the sun.

> **DUKE V/O**
> All energy flows according to the
> whims of the Great Magnet.

C/U Barrel of the gun. It fires. An explosion of desert
dirt.

> **DUKE V/O**
> What a fool I was to defy Him.

The IGUANA sits unfazed.

> **DUKE V/O**
> Never cross the Great Magnet.
> I understood this now...

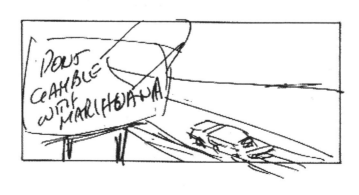

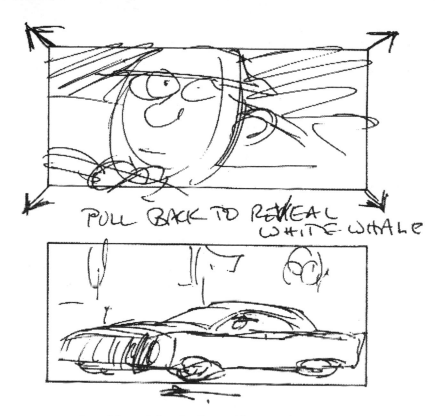

PULL BACK TO REVEAL WHITE WHALE

(another blast from the gun)
... and with understanding came a
sense of almost terminal relief.

DUKE stands alone in the vast desert firing at nothing,
the thuds of the explosions echo away.

EXT. ROAD INTO VEGAS — DAY

The RED SHARK driving back towards Las Vegas.

> **DUKE V/O**
> I had to get rid of The Shark. Too
> many people might recognize it....
> ... especially the Vegas Police.
>   (tight C/U of DUKE)
> Luckily, my credit card was still
> technically valid.

PULL BACK TO REVEAL:

DUKE, now driving a white Cadillac Coupe de Ville — THE
WHITE WHALE.

DUKE pushes buttons — lowers the top.

DUKE V/O

This was a superior machine — ten
grand worth of gimmicks and high
price special effects. The rear windows leapt up with a touch like frogs
in a dynamited pond. The dashboard
was full of esoteric lights and dials
and meters that I would never understand.

EXT. FLAMINGO HOTEL — AFTERNOON

A GIANT SIGN: THE FLAMINGO WELCOMES THE NATIONAL DA'S CON-
FERENCE ON NARCOTICS & DANGEROUS DRUGS.

DUKE V/O

If the Pigs were gathering in Vegas,
I felt the Drug Culture should be
represented as well ... and there was
a certain bent appeal in the notion
of running a savage burn on one Las

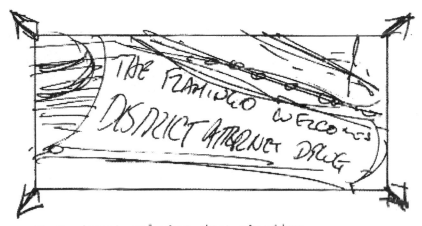

Vegas hotel and then just wheeling
across town and checking into another.

The WHITE WHALE turns into a VIP parking slot, immediately
attended by impressed MINIONS.

> **DUKE V/O**
> Me and a thousand ranking cops from
> all over America. Why not? Move con-
> fidently into their midst.

INT. FLAMINGO HOTEL LOBBY — AFTERNOON

DUKE enters — old Levis, grubby sneakers, 10 peso Acapulco
shirt coming apart at the seams, 3 day growth, eyes hid-
den behind mirror shades. He heads for the check-in line.

> **DUKE V/O**
> My arrival was badly timed.

THE PLACE IS FULL OF COPS. 200 of them, on vacation, all

137

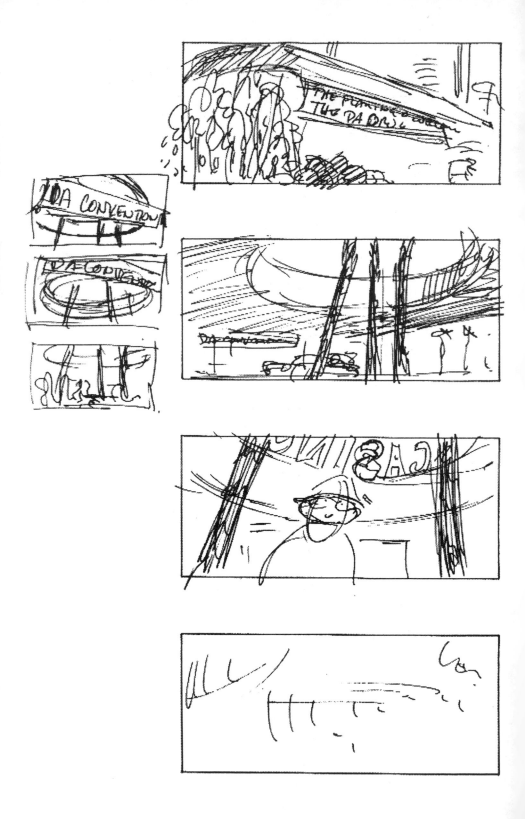

dressed in cut price Vegas casuals: plaid Bermuda shorts,
Arnie Palmer golf shirts, and rubberized beach sandals.

Ahead of DUKE — A POLICE CHIEF argues with the DESK
CLERK. The POLICE CHIEF'S AGNEW STYLE WIFE stands to the
side, weeping. The POLICE CHIEF'S FRIENDS stand uneasily
around.

> ### POLICE CHIEF
> What do you mean I'm too late to reg-
> ister? I'm a police chief. From
> Michigan. Look, fella, I told you.
> (waves a POSTCARD)
> I have a postcard here that says I
> have reservations in this hotel.

> ### CLERK
> (prissily)
> I'm sorry, sir. You're on the "late
> list." Your reservations were trans-
> ferred to the ... ah ... Moonlight
> Motel, which is out on Paradise
> Boulevard....

> ### POLICE CHIEF
> I've already paid for my goddamn
> room!

> ### CLERK
> It's actually a very fine place of
> lodging and only sixteen blocks from
> here, with its own pool and ...

> ### POLICE CHIEF
> You dirty little faggot! Call the
> manager! I'm tired of listening to
> this dogshit!

FRIENDS restrain the POLICE CHIEF.

> ### CLERK
> (solicitously)
> I'm so sorry, sir. May I call you a
> cab?

The POLICE CHIEF's screamed insults fade away...

> ### DUKE V/O
> Of course, I could hear what the

Sc 76

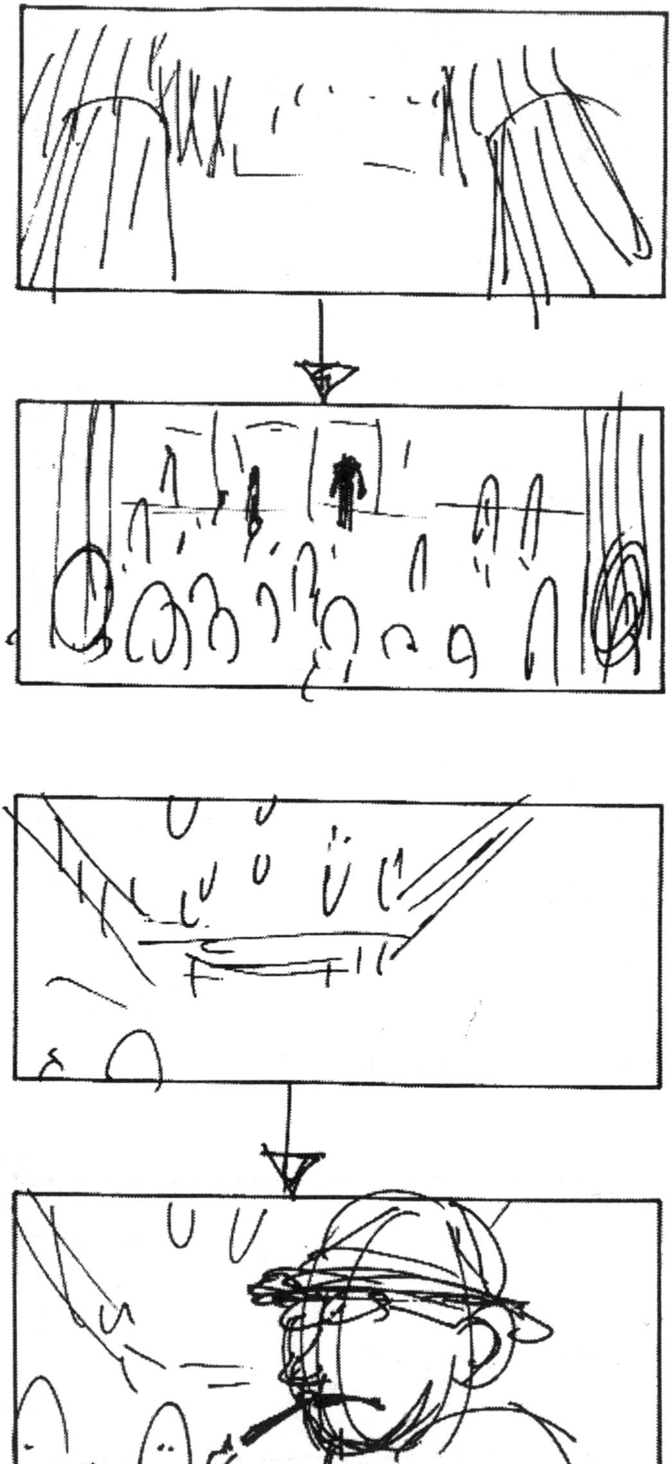

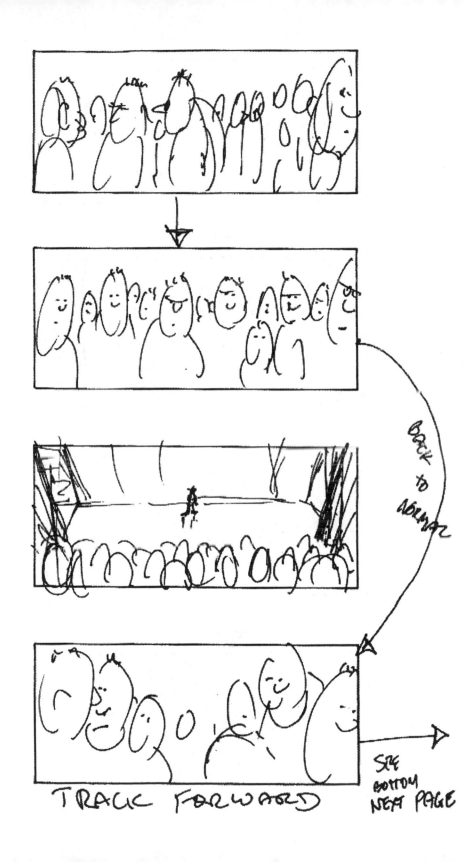

BACK to NORMAL

TRACK FORWARD

SEE
BOTTOM
NEXT PAGE

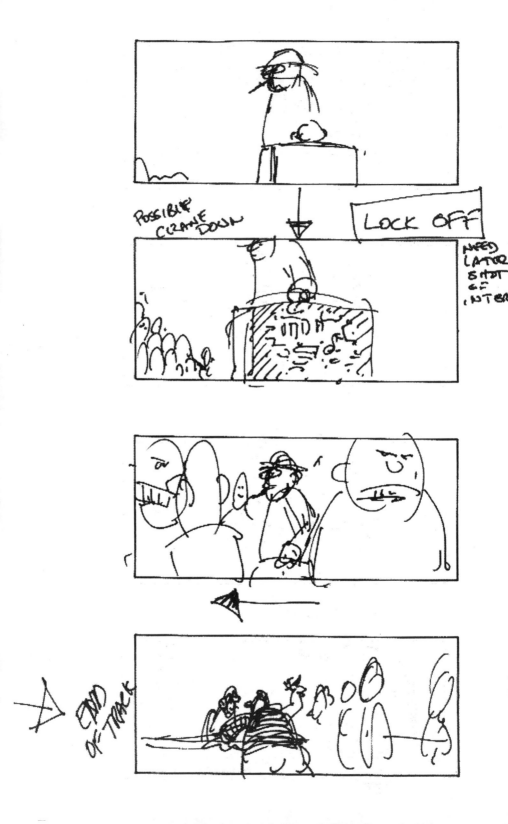

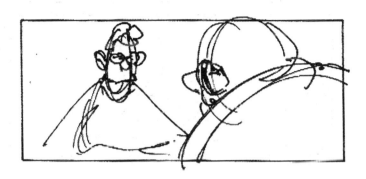

POP DRUG
CASE IN
FRONT OF
COP

Clerk was really saying..

CLERK
(IN DUKE'S IMAGINATION)
Listen, you fuzzy little shithead—
I've been fucked around, in my time,
by a fairly good cross-section of
mean- tempered rule-crazy cops and
now it's MY turn. "Fuck you, officer,
I'm in charge here, and I'm telling
you we don't have room for you."

DUKE steps to the desk, around the raging POLICE CHIEF.

DUKE
Say. I hate to interrupt, but I won-
der if maybe I could just sort of
slide through and get out of your
way. Name's Duke — Raoul Duke. My
attorney made the reservation.

DUKE snaps a credit card down onto the counter. EVERYONE
goes silent. The POLICE CHIEF GROUP stares at him like he

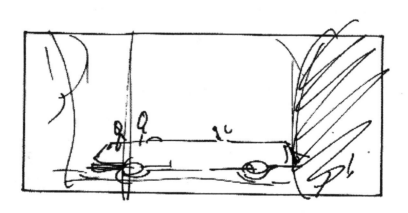

was some kind of water rat crawling up to the desk. The
CLERK — hits the bell for the BELLBOY.

CLERK
Certainly, Mr. Duke!

DUKE
My bags are out there in that white

                    Cadillac convertible. Can you have
                    someone drive it around to the room?

ALL EYES turn to the gleaming WHITE WHALE.

                              DUKE
                    Oh, and could I get a quart of Wild
                    Turkey, two fifths of Baccardi, and a
                    night's worth of ice delivered to my
                    room, please?

                              CLERK
                    Don't worry about a thing, sir. Just
                    enjoy your stay.

                              DUKE
                    Well, thank you.

DUKE gives the POLICE CHIEF a polite smile — crosses to
the elevator — turns to face the GAWPING COPS — pops a
can of beer and toasts them. The doors close.

INT. HOTEL FLAMINGO — CORRIDOR OUTSIDE SUITE — DAY

DUKE rams the key home — swings the door open.

                              DUKE
                    Ah, home at last!

INT. HOTEL FLAMINGO SUITE — AFTERNOON

DUKE enters. The door hits something with a thud.

A 16-year old GIRL with the aura of an angry Pit Bull.

GONZO stands in the bathroom doorway — stark naked with a
drug-addled grin on his face.

                              DUKE
                    You degenerate pig!

                              GONZO
                    It can't be helped. This is Lucy.
                              (laughing distractedly)
                    You know—like "Lucy In The Sky With
                    Diamonds."

LUCY eyes DUKE venomously.

                              145

GONZO

Lucy! Lucy, be cool, goddamnit!
Remember what happened at the airport! No more of that, okay?

LUCY keeps her eyes on DUKE. GONZO idles over and puts
his arm round her shoulder.

GONZO

Lucy ... this is my <u>client</u>. This is
Mr. Duke, the famous journalist. He's
<u>paying</u> for this suite, Lucy. He's on
<u>our</u> side.

DUKE flops onto the sofa.

GONZO

Mr. Duke is my <u>friend</u>. He loves
artists.

DUKE notices for the first time that the room is full of
artwork. Maybe 40 or 50 portraits, some in oil, some in
charcoal, all more or less the same size and same face.

GONZO

Lucy paints portraits of Barbra
Streisand.

LUCY

I drew these from TV.

GONZO

Fantastic. She came all the way down
here from Montana just to give these
portraits to Barbra. We're going over
to the Americana Hotel tonight to
meet her backstage ...

DUKE's voice rises above GONZO.

DUKE V/O

I desperately needed <u>peace</u>, rest,
sanctuary. I hadn't counted on this.
Finding my attorney on acid and
locked into some kind of preternatur-
al courtship.

DUKE

Well, I guess they brought the car

146

round by now. LET'S GET THE STUFF OUT
OF THE TRUNK.

DUKE fixes GONZO hard.

> **GONZO**
> Absolutely, LET'S GET THE STUFF.
> (to LUCY)
> Now, we'll be right back. Don't
> answer the phone if it rings.

> **LUCY**
> (makes one-fingered
> Jesus freak sign)
> God bless.

INT. FLAMINGO HOTEL — CORRIDOR OUTSIDE SUITE — DAY

DUKE collars GONZO — serious.

> **DUKE**
> WELL? What are your plans?

> **GONZO**
> Plans?

> **DUKE**
> Lucy.

> **GONZO**
> (struggling to focus)
> Shit. I met her on the plane and I
> had all that acid.
> (he shrugs)
> You know, those little blue barrels.
> I gave her a cap before I realized
> ... she's a religious freak....
> Jesus, she's never even had a <u>drink</u>.

> **DUKE**
> Well ... It'll probably work out. We
> can keep her loaded and peddle her
> ass at the drug convention.

GONZO stares uneasily at DUKE.

> **GONZO**
> Listen, she's running away from home
> for something like the fifth time in

147

six months. It's terrible.

> **DUKE**
> She's perfect for this gig. These
> cops will go fifty bucks a head to
> beat her into submission and then
> gang fuck her. We can set her up in
> one of these back street motels, hang
> pictures of Jesus all over the room,
> then turn these pigs loose on her ...
> Hell she's strong; she'll hold her
> own.

GONZO'S face twitches badly.

> **GONZO**
> Jesus Christ. I knew you were sick
> but I never expected to hear you
> actually say that kind of stuff.

> **DUKE**
> It's straight economics. This girl is
> a god-send. Shit, she can make us a
> grand a day.

> **GONZO**
> NO! Stop talking like that.

> **DUKE**
> I figure she can do about four at a
> time. Christ, if we keep her full of
> acid that's more like two grand a
> day. Maybe three.

> **GONZO**
> You filthy bastard. I should cave
> your fucking head in.

> **DUKE**
> In a few hours, she'll probably be
> sane enough to work herself into a
> towering Jesus-based rage at the hazy
> recollection of being seduced by some
> kind of cruel Samoan who fed her
> liquor and LSD, dragged her to a
> Vegas hotel room and savagely pene-
> trated every orifice in her body with
> his throbbing, uncircumcised member.

GONZO starts crying.

> **GONZO**
> NO! I felt <u>sorry</u> for the girl, I
> wanted to help her!

> **DUKE**
> You'll go straight to the gas cham-
> ber. And even if you manage to beat
> <u>that</u>, they'll send you back to Nevada
> for Rape and Consensual Sodomy. She's
> got to go.

Pause.

> **GONZO**
> Shit, it doesn't pay to try to help
> somebody these days.

A silence.

> **DUKE V/O**
> The only alternative was to take her
> out to the desert and feed her
> remains to the lizards. But, it
> seemed a bit heavy for the thing we
> were trying to protect: My attorney.

> **GONZO**
> We have to cut her loose. She's got
> two hundred dollars. And we can
> always call the cops up there in
> Montana, where she lives, and turn
> her in.

> **DUKE**
> What? ... What kind of goddamn mon-
> ster are you?

> **GONZO**
> It just occurred to me, that she has
> no witnesses. Anything that she says
> about us is completely worthless

> **DUKE**
> Us?

INT. HOTEL FLAMINGO SUITE — SUNSET

DUKE is speaking into the phone in hushed tones.

> DUKE
> Hotel Americana? I need a reserva-
> tion. For my niece. Listen, I need
> her treated very gently. She's an
> artist, and might seem a trifle high-
> strung....

In the background GONZO helps LUCY and her paintings out
the door.

> GONZO
> Okay, Lucy, it's time to go meet
> Barbra...

> DUKE V/O
> I felt like a Nazi, but it had to be
> done.

[INT. HOTEL FLAMINGO SUITE — A FEW MINUTES LATER

OMITTED]

EXT. ON THE STREETS — A CAB STAND — DUSK

The WHITE WHALE pulls up - DUKE at the wheel. GONZO helps
LUCY and her paintings from the car. .

> DUKE V/O
> Lucy was a potentially fatal mill-
> stone on both our necks. There was
> absolutely no choice but to cut her
> adrift and hope her memory was
> fucked.

GONZO unrolls a couple of bills — pays off a CAB DRIVER —
waves to LUCY in the back with her paintings. She's
starting to come down....

GONZO gets back in the WHITE WHALE and slaps his hands
together as if washing his hands of the situation.

> GONZO
> Well that's that. Take off slowly.
> Don't attract attention.

They pull out into traffic.

EXT. LAS VEGAS STREETS — DUSK

> **GONZO**
> I gave the cabbie an extra ten bucks
> to make sure she gets there safe.
> Also, I told him I'd be there myself
> in an hour, and if she wasn't, I'd
> come back out here and rip his lungs
> out.

> **DUKE**
> That's good. You can't be subtle in
> this town.

> **GONZO**
> As your attorney, I advise you to
> tell me where you put the goddamn
> mescaline.

> **DUKE**
> Maybe we should take it easy tonight.

> **GONZO**
> Right. Let's find a good seafood
> restaurant and eat some red salmon. I
> feel a powerful lust for red
> salmon....

The electric WHITE WHALE heads off down the Strip. The
sun's going down behind the scrub hills, a good
Kristofferson tune croaks on the radio in the warm dusk.

INT. HOTEL FLAMINGO SUITE — BATHROOM — NEXT MORNING

GONZO throws up in the toilet bowl.

In the background, DUKE opens curtains. Daylight blinds
him.

> **DUKE**
> Come on, we're going to be late.

GONZO looks up at his sick reflection — wipes his mouth
with a towel.

> **GONZO**
> This goddamn mescaline. Why the fuck

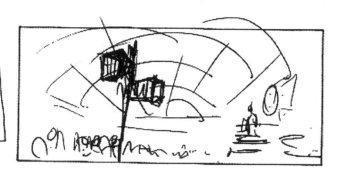

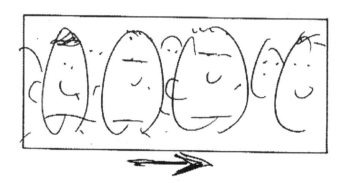

RAOUL DUKE
PRIVATE INVESTIGATOR

TILT UP

can't they make it a little less
pure? Maybe mix it up with Rolaids or
something.

INT. HOTEL BALLROOM — DAY

                    EXECUTIVE DIRECTOR
            (crackling and booming over
              the lousy sound system)
On behalf of the prosecuting attor-
neys of this county, I welcome you to
the Third National DA's Conference on
Narcotics and Dangerous Drugs.

Th EXECUTIVE DIRECTOR — well groomed, GOP businessman type
— speaks from the podium. A banner behind him reads:
NATIONAL DA'S CONVENTION 1971. "If You Don't Know, Come To
Learn...If You Know, Come To Teach."

A BIG MIXED CROWD: TOP LEVEL STRAIGHT COPS, UNDERCOVER
NARCS AND OTHER TWILIGHT TYPES — beards, mustaches and
super-Mod dress. Just because you're a cop, doesn't mean
you can't be WITH IT! However, for ever URBAN-HIPSTER
there are around 20 REDNECKS.

A dozen big, low-fidelity speakers mounted on steel poles

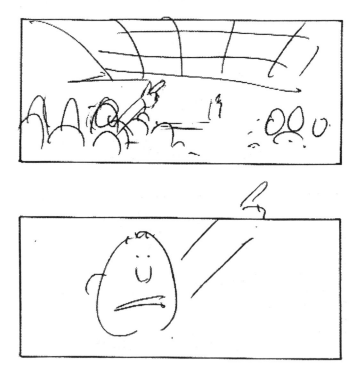

distort and feed back the EXECUTIVE's voice through the room.

At the back, under a loudspeaker, sits DUKE — $40 FBI wingtips, a Pat Boone madras sportcoat, and an official name tag: RAOUL DUKE, PRIVATE INVESTIGATOR, L.A.

GONZO sits beside him. His name tag: DR. GONZO. EXPERT, CRIMINAL DRUG ANALYSIS. He's nervous — close to the edge.

> **GONZO**
> (lowers his voice)
> I saw these bastards in Easy Rider,
> but I didn't believe they were real.
> Not like this. Not hundreds of them!

> **DUKE**
> They're actually nice people when you
> get to know them.

> **GONZO**
> Man, I know these people in my god-
> damn blood!

> **DUKE**
> Don't mention that word around here.

L. RON BLUMPQUISTER

GONZO LEAVES

You'll get them excited.

                    GONZO
This is a fucking nightmare.

                    DUKE
Right. Sure as hell some dope-dealing
bomb freak is going to recognize you
and put the word out that you're par-
tying with a thousand cops.

                COP IN BACK
SSSSHHH!

DR. BLUMQUIST — a "drug expert" — takes the stage.

                DR. BLUMQUIST
We must come to terms with the Drug
Culture in the country ... country
... country ...

The sound systems echoes.

            DR. BLUMQUIST (CONT'D)
The reefer butt is called a "roach,"
because it resembles a cockroach ...
cockroach ... cockroach ...

                    GONZO
                  (whispers)
What the fuck are these people talking about? You'd have to be crazy on
acid to think a joint looked like a
goddamn cockroach!

                  DUKE V/O
It was clear that we had stumbled
into a prehistoric gathering.

                DR. BLUMQUIST
Now, there are four states of being
in the cannabis, or marijuana, soci-
ety: Cool, Groovy, Hip, and Square.
The square is seldom if ever cool. He
is not "with it," that is, he doesn't
know "what's happening." But if he
manages to figure it out, he moves up
a notch to "hip."

DUKE and GONZO listen in disbelief.

>   **DR. BLUMQUIST (CONT'D)**
> And if he can bring himself to
> approve of what is happening, he
> becomes "groovy." After that, with
> much luck and perseverance, he can
> rise to the rank of "cool." A cool
> guy ... cool guy ... cool guy ...

>   **COP IN BACK**
> Dr. Bloomquist, do you think the
> anthropologist, Margaret Mead's
> strange behavior of late might possi-
> bly be explained by a private mari-
> juana addiction?

>   **DR. BLUMQUIST**
> I really don't know, but at her age,
> if she did smoke grass, she'd have
> one hell of a trip!

Roars of laughter.

LIGHTS DOWN

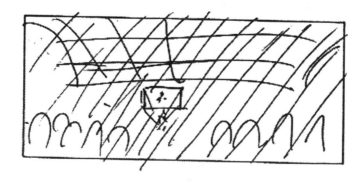

157

REEFER MADNESS

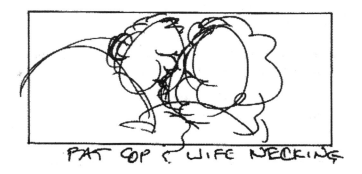

PAT COP & WIFE NECKING

GONZO
I know a hell of a lot better ways to
waste my time than listening to this
bullshit.

He stands, knocking the ashtray off his chair arm, and
plunges down the aisle to the door.

COP IN BACK
Down in front!

GONZO
Fuck you! I have to get <u>out</u>! I don't
<u>belong</u> here!

COP IN BACK
Good riddance!

He stumbles from the room. DUKE turns his attention back
to the stage.

The lights go down. A black & white film — REEFER MAD-
NESS! — illustrates his now evangelical talk.

FILM NARRATOR
KNOW YOUR DOPE FIEND! YOUR LIFE MAY
DEPEND ON IT!

You will not be able to see his eyes
because of Tea-Shades, but his knuckles will be white from inner tension...

DUKE turns his attention to a 340 pound TEXAN POLICE
CHIEF who necks with his 290 pound WIFE beside him.

                    FILM NARRATOR
    ... and his pants will be crusted
with semen from constantly jacking
off when he can't find a rape
victim ...

DUKE gazes at the TEXAN and his WIFE. — Feigning sick-
ness, he gets up, hand over mouth.

                        DUKE
Pardon me, I feel sick.

                    FILM NARRATOR
He will stagger and babble when ques-
tioned. He will not respect your
badge. The Dope Fiend fears nothing.
He will attack, for no reason, with
every weapon at his command — includ
ing yours ...

DUKE heads for the exit.

> ### DUKE
> Sorry, sick ... Beg pardon! Feeling
> sick...

> ### FILM NARRATOR
> BEWARE. Any officer apprehending a
> suspected marijuana addict should use
> all necessary force immediately. One
> stitch in time (on him) will usually
> save nine on you.

DUKE CRASHES OUT THROUGH THE DOOR.

INT. CASINO BAR — DAY

DUKE sees GONZO at the bar — talking to a SPORTY LOOKING
COP about 40 whose name tag identifies him as a DISTRICT
ATTORNEY FROM GEORGIA.

> ### DA
> I'm a whiskey man myself. We don't
> have much trouble from drugs where I
> come from....

> ### GONZO
> You will. One of these nights you'll
> wake up and find a junkie tearing
> your bedroom apart.

> ### DA
> Naw!

> ### GONZO
> They'll climb right into your bedroom
> and sit on your chest with big Bowie
> knives. They might even sit on your
> wife's chest. Put the blade right
> down on her throat.

> ### DA
> Not down in my parts

DUKE joins them.

> ### DUKE
> (to WAITRESS)
> Rum and ice, please.

                    DA
          (looks at DUKE'S NAME TAG)
You're another one of these
California boys. Your friend here's
been tellin' us about dope fiends.

                  DUKE

They're everywhere. Nobody's safe.
And sure as hell not in the South.
They like warm weather....
You'd never believe it. In L.A. it's
out of control. First it was drugs,
now it's witchcraft.

                    DA
Witchcraft? Shit, you can't mean it!

The BARTENDER cleans his glasses, one ear straining for
the conversation.

                  GONZO
Read the newspapers.

                  DUKE
Man, you don't know trouble until you
have to face down a bunch of these
addicts gone crazy for human sacri-
tice!

                    DA
Naw! That's science fiction stuff!

                  DUKE
Not where we operate.

                  GONZO
Hell, in Malibu alone, these goddamn
Satan worshippers kill six or eight
people <u>every day</u>. All they want is
the blood. They'll take people right
off the street if they have to.

                  DUKE
Just the other day we had a case
where they grabbed a girl right out
of a McDonald's hamburger stand. She
was a waitress, about sixteen years
old ... with a lot of people watching, too!

                    161

The BARTENDER keeps cleaning the same glass — more and more furiously.

>   DA
>   What happened? What did they do to
>   her?

>   GONZO
>   Do? Jesus Christ, man. They chopped
>   her goddamn head off right there in
>   the parking lot! Then they cut all
>   kinds of holes in her head and sucked
>   out the blood!

>   DA
>   (DA ad-libs a summation
>   of the crime)
>   And nobody did anything?

>   DUKE
>   What could they do? The guy that took
>   the head was about six-seven, and
>   maybe three-hundred pounds. He was
>   packing two Lugers, and the others
>   had M-16s.

>   GONZO
>   They just ran back out into Death
>   Valley — you know, where Manson
>   turned up ...

>   DUKE
>   Like big lizards.

>   GONZO
>   ... and every one of them stark
>   naked....

>   DA
>   Naked!?

>   DUKE
>   Naked.

>   GONZO
>   Yeh, naked!... except for the
>   weapons.

                        DUKE
        They were all veterans.

                          DA
        Veterans?!!!?

Agog with the horrors of the story, the BARTENDER polishes
the glass — faster and faster ...

                        GONZO
        Yeh. The big guy used to be a major
        in the Marines.

                          DA
        A major!

                        GONZO
        We know where he lives, but we can't
        get near the house.

                          DA
        Naw! Not a major.

                        GONZO
        He wanted the pineal gland.

                          DA
        Really?

                        GONZO
        That's how he got so big. When he
        quit the Marines he was just a little
        guy.

                        DUKE
        Usually it's whole families. During
        the night. Most of them don't even
        wake up until they feel their heads
        going — and then, of course, it's too
        late.

The glass smashes in the BARTENDER's hand.

                   DUKE (cont'd)
        Happens every day.

DUKE turns to a WAITRESS with a warm smile.

                    DUKE (CONT'D)
Three more rums. Plenty of ice. Maybe
a handful of lime chunks.

                    WAITRESS
Are you guys with the police convention upstairs?

                       DA
We sure are, Miss.

                    WAITRESS
I thought so. I never heard that kind
of talk around here before. Jesus
Christ! How do you guys <u>stand</u> that
kind of work?

                     GONZO
                    (grinning)
We <u>like</u> it. It's groovy.

The WAITRESS stares — sickened — at GONZO.

                      DUKE
What's wrong with you? Hell, <u>somebody</u>
has to do it.

                     GONZO
Hurry up with those drinks. We're
thirsty. Only two rums. Make mine a
Bloody Mary.

                       DA
                (whacks his fist
                  on the bar)
Hell, I really hate to hear this.
Because everything that happens in
California seems to get down our way,
sooner or later. Mostly Atlanta. But
that was back when the goddamn bas-
tards were <u>peaceful</u>. All we had to do
was to keep 'em under surveillance.
They didn't roam around much..But now
Jesus, it seems <u>nobody's</u> safe.

                     GONZO
              (with a conspiratorial nod)
You're going to need to take the bull

by the horns — go to the mat with
this scum.

                    DA
What do you mean by that?

                  GONZO
You <u>know</u> what I mean. We've done it
before and we can damn well do it
again!

                  DUKE
Cut their goddamn heads off. Every
one of them. That's what we're doing
in California.

                    DA
              (stupified)
WHAT?

                  GONZO
Sure. It's all on the Q.T., but
everybody who matters is with us all
the way down the line.

                  DUKE
We keep it quiet. It's not the kind
of thing you'd want to talk about
upstairs. Not with the press around.

                    DA
            (recovering slightly)
Hell, no. We'd never hear the goddamn
end of it.

                  DUKE
Dobermans don't talk.

                    DA
What?

                  GONZO
Sometimes it's easier to just rip out
the backstraps.

                  DUKE
They'll fight like hell if you try to
take the head without the dogs.

                              DA
        God almighty!
                    (muttering in a daze)
        I don't think I should tell my wife
        about this. She'd never understand.
        You know how women are.

DUKE gives the DA a brotherly slap on the back.

                             DUKE
        Just be thankful your heart is young
        and strong.

DUKE and GONZO leave the stunned DA — staring into the
swirling ice in drink.

INT. HOTEL FLAMINGO SUITE — DAY

DUKE and GONZO fall into the suite in fits of laughter.

GONZO feels the nausea rise suddenly — heads for the
bathroom. Immediate sounds of retching.

The phone message light is blinking. DUKE opens a beer,
picks up the phone.

                             DUKE
        What's the message? My light is
        blinking.

                          CLERK V/O
        Ah, yes. Mr. Duke? You have one mes-
        sage: "Call Lucy at the Americana
        Hotel, room 1600."

                             DUKE
        Holy shit!

DUKE slams the phone down. GONZO emerges from the bathroom
— looking like death.

                             DUKE
        Lucy called.

GONZO sags visibly — like an animal taking a bullet.

                            GONZO
        What?

The telephone rings. DUKE answers.

                              166

INT. FLAMINGO HOTEL — RECEPTION — DAY

A worried CLERK speaks in to the phone.

> **CLERK**
> Mr. Duke? Hello, Mr. Duke, I'm sorry
> we were cut off a moment ago ... I
> thought I should call again, because
> I was wondering ...

INT. FLAMINGO HOTEL SUITE — DAY

> **DUKE**
> WHAT?
> > (hand over the PHONE)
> What has that crazy bitch said to
> him?
> > (screams)
> There's a war on, man! People are
> being killed!

> **CLERK V/O**
> Killed?

> **DUKE**
> IN VIETNAM! ON THE GODDAMN TELEVI-
> SION!

> **CLERK V/O**
> Oh ... yes ... yes ... This terrible
> war. When will it end?

> **DUKE**
> Tell me. What do you want?

In the background GONZO is upturning a sofa to retrieve
his stash from the lining.

> **CLERK V/O**
> The woman who left that message for
> you sounded very disturbed. I think
> she was crying...

> **DUKE**
> Crying? Why was she crying?

> **CLERK V/O**
> Well, uh. She didn't say Mr. Duke.
> But since I know you're here with the

Police Convention....

                    DUKE
Look, you want to be gentle with that
woman if she ever calls again. We're
watching her very carefully.... this
woman has been into laudanum. It's a
controlled experiment, but I suspect
we'll need your cooperation before
this thing is over.

                  CLERK V/O
                 (hesitantly)
Well, certainly.... We're always
happy to cooperate with the police...

                    DUKE
Don't worry. You're protected. Just
treat this poor woman like you'd
treat any other human being in trouble.

                  CLERK V/O
What? Ah...yes, yes, I see what you
mean...Yes...so, <u>you'll</u> be responsible
then?

                    DUKE
Of course. And now I have to get back
to the news. Send up some ice.

He hangs up. GONZO zaps TV channels — commercials.

                   GONZO
Good work. They'll treat us like goddamn lepers after that.

                    DUKE
              (slowly, carefully)
Lucy is looking for you.

                   GONZO
                 (laughing)
No, she's looking for <u>you</u>.

                    DUKE
Me?

                              GONZO
          She really flipped over you. The only
          way I could get rid of her was by
          saying you were taking me out to the
          desert for a showdown — that you
          wanted me out of the way so you could
          have her all to yourself.
                          (laughing again)
          I guess she figures you won. That
          phone message wasn't for _me_, was it?

A look of stunned realization from DUKE ...

INT. FANTASY COURT ROOM — DAY

LUCY is on the witness stand.

                              LUCY
          Yessir, those two men in the dock are
          the ones who gave me the LSD and took
          me to the hotel.

A doomed DUKE and GONZO await their fate.

                              LUCY
          I don't know for sure what they done
          to me, but I remember it was horri-
          ble.

                              JUDGE
          Twenty years ... and Double
          Castration!

The JUDGE bangs his gavel.

INT. HOTEL FLAMINGO SUITE — DAY

DUKE is madly stuffing his suitcase.

                              GONZO
          Wait! You can't leave me alone in
          this snake pit. This room is in _my_
          name.

DUKE KEEPS PACKING. GONZO is looking worried.

                              GONZO
          OK, goddamnit!.... Look...I'll _call_
          her. I'll get her off our backs.

                                169

You're right. She's my problem.

                    DUKE
It's gone too far.

                    GONZO
Relax. Let me handle this.
          (dials the PHONE, snaps
              angrily at DUKE)
You'd make a piss-poor lawyer.
... Room 1600, please.
              (to DUKE)
As your attorney, I advise you not to
worry.
          (nods towards bathroom)
Take a hit out of that little brown
bottle in my shaving kit.

DUKE goes in the bathroom. He finds a little bottle — a
label: "DRINK ME".

                    DUKE
What is this?

                    GONZO
You won't need much. Just a little
<u>tiny</u> taste, that stuff makes pure
mescaline seem like ginger-beer.
Adrenochrome.

DUKE stares wonderingly at the bottle.

                    DUKE
Adrenochrome ...

                    GONZO
              (into PHONE)
Hi, Lucy? Yeah, it's me. I got your
message...what? Hell, no, I taught
the bastard a lesson he'll never for-
get... what? No, not dead, but he
won't be bothering anybody for a
while. Yeah. I left him out there, I
stomped him, then pulled all his
teeth out....

                    DUKE V/O
I remember thinking, "Jesus, what a
terrible thing to lay on somebody

170

with a head full of acid".

DUKE dips a match head into the brown bottle — studies it — TASTES IT — NOTHING — TASTES SOME MORE ...

GONZO
(to PHONE)

But here's the problem. That bastard cashed a bad check downstairs and gave you as a reference. They'll be looking for both of you. Yeah, I know, but you can't judge a book by its cover, Lucy. Some people are just basically rotten... Anyway, the last thing you want to do is call this hotel again; they'll trace the call and put you straight behind bars ... no, I'm moving to the Tropicana right away. I have to go, they've got the phone tapped. Yeah, I know, it was horrible, but it's all over now ... OH MY GOD! THEY'RE KICKING THE DOOR DOWN!

(throws the PHONE
down; shouts)

No! Get away from me! I'm innocent! It was Duke! I swear to God!

(stomps the PHONE; moans)

No, I don't know where she is. You'll never catch Lucy! She's gone! I swear, I don't know where she is! DON'T PUT THAT THING ON ME!

(slams the PHONE down)

GONZO sits back in his chair ... watching MISSION IMPOSSIBLE.

GONZO

Well. That's that. She's probably stuffing herself down the incinerator about now. That's the last we should be hearing from Lucy.

(fumbling with the
hash pipe)

Where's the opium?

DUKE stares at the back of GONZO's neck. SOMETHING VERY STRANGE IS HAPPENING TO HIM....

                    DUKE V/O

I remember slumping on the bed, his
performance had given me a bad jolt.
For a moment I thought his mind had
snapped — that he actually believed
he was being attacked by invisible
enemies. But the room was quiet
again.

DUKE CLUTCHES THE BROWN BOTTLE.

                    DUKE

Where'd you get this?

                    GONZO

Never mind, it's absolutely pure.

                    DUKE

Jesus ... what kind of monster client
have you picked up this time? There's
only one source for this stuff — the
adrenaline gland from a living human
body!

GONZO turns to smile at DUKE.

                    GONZO

I know, but the guy didn't have any
cash to pay me. He's one of these
Satanism freaks. He offered me human
blood — said it would take me higher
than I've ever been in my life.
              (laughs — struts round
              DUKE — eyes bright with
              expectation)
I thought he was kidding, so I told
him I'd just as soon have an ounce or
so of pure adrenochrome — or maybe
just a fresh adrenaline gland to chew
on.

                    DUKE V/O

I could already feel the stuff working on me — the first wave felt like
a combination of mescaline and
methedrine — maybe I should take a
swim, I thought ...

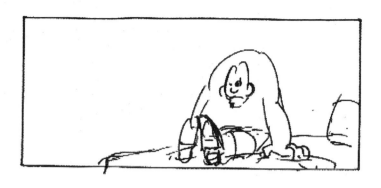

SMOKE OOZING FROM
GONZO'S CHAIR

TRACK/
ZOOM

OR
JAGGED
CUTTING

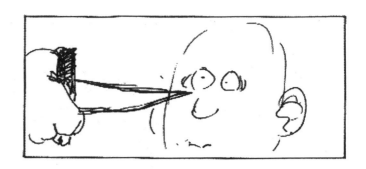

TWO STAGES

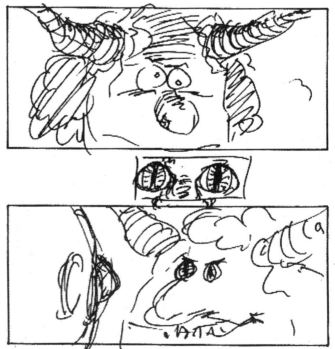

SHOE BURSTING

SPLIT HAIR ESCAPES

WALL PAPER FLAME PROJECTIO

SMOKE IN ROOM

C/U SHIRT
BURSTING
OUT

BED SHAKING

CONTACT
LENS
FOR
DUKE

FLAME

BLUE SCREEN

BLEEDING
from the
eye

QUIVERING MADLY

TRY ZOOM/TRACK AS GONZO WALKS AWAY

EVERY THING SHAKING

START TIPPING CAMERA

DUKE sees that GONZO is TOYING WITH HIS HUNTING KNIFE ...

> **GONZO**
> Yeah, they nailed this guy for child
> molesting. He swore he didn't do it.
> "Why should I fuck with <u>children</u>?" he
> says. "They're too <u>small</u>." Christ,
> what could I say? Even a goddamn
> werewolf is entitled to legal coun-
> sel. I didn't dare turn the creep
> down. He might have picked up a let-
> ter opener and gone after my pineal
> gland!

GONZO JABS WITH THE RAZOR BRIGHT KNIFE. DUKE'S BODY IS
GOING RIGID — HE SPEAKS THROUGH GRITTED TEETH.

> **DUKE**
> Why not? We should get some of that.
> Just eat a big handful and see what
> happens.

> **GONZO**
> Some of what?

> **DUKE**
> (spitting words)
> Extract of pineal!

> **GONZO**
> (STARING AT DUKE WITH
> A STRANGE SMILE)
> Sure. That's a <u>good</u> idea. One whiff
> of that shit would turn you into
> something out of a goddamn medical
> encyclopedia.

GONZO GROWS HORNS — HIS FACE BECOMES A MEXICAN DEMON
MASK.

> **GONZO**
> Man, your head would swell up like a
> watermelon, you'd probably gain about
> a hundred pounds in two hours...

A CLOVEN HOOF BURSTS THROUGH GONZO'S SHOE.

> **DUKE**
> Right!

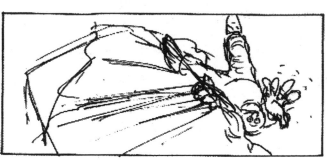

POSSIBLY SUPER IN POST

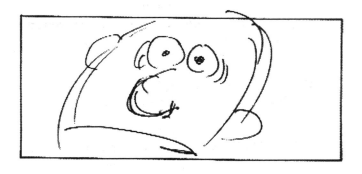

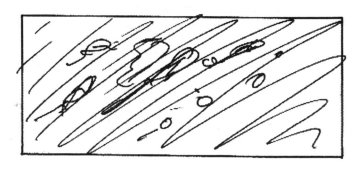

                              GONZO
          ... grow claws ... bleeding warts.

GONZO'S CHEST EXPANDS — BONY RIBS BURSTING HIS SHIRT.

                              DUKE
          Yes!

                              GONZO
          ... then you'd notice about six huge
          hairy tits swelling up on your back
          ...

A TAIL LASHES, HOOFS STRIKE THE FLOOR. GONZO TOWERS — A
FLAME RED DEMON!

                              DUKE
          Fantastic!

DUKE is now so wired that his hands are CLAWING UNCON-
TROLLABLY at the bedspread, JERKING IT RIGHT OUT FROM
UNDER HIM. His heels are dug into the mattress with both
KNEES LOCKED, EYEBALLS SWELLING.

GONZO-DEMON LOOMS AGAINST THE CEILING.

                              GONZO
          you'd go blind ... your body would
          turn to wax ... they'd have to put
          you in a wheelbarrow and ...

GONZO'S VOICE FADES AWAY — DUKE'S frenzied gaze reveals
GONZO REVERTED TO NORMAL HUMAN SHAPE AND SIZE.

                              GONZO
          Man I'll try about anything; but I'd
          never touch a pineal gland.

                              DUKE
          FINISH THE FUCKING STORY! What hap-
          pened?! What about the glands?

GONZO, a small smile on his lips, backs away warily ...
towards the TV — NOW A HUNDRED FEET AWAY IN THE DISTANCE ...

                              GONZO
          Jesus, that stuff got right on top of
          you, didn't it.

VEINS stand out on DUKE's forehead. He is purplish-red.
OVER THE TOP! Too late, he realizes he is NEAR DEATH!

                    DUKE
          Maybe you could just ... shove me
          into the pool, or something ...

GONZO shakes his head disgustedly.

                    GONZO
          If I put you in the pool right now,
          you'd sink like a goddamn stone. You
          took too much. Jesus, look at your
          face, you're about to explode.

GONZO sits back down ... watching the TV.

                    GONZO
          Don't try and fight it, or you'll get
          brain bubbles. Strokes, aneurysms.
          You'll just wither up and die.

DUKE FALLS TO THE GROUND, WRITHING, CATATONIC, SINKING
INTO PARALYSIS.

AND THE SOUND, SUDDENLY AND STRANGELY, OF THE VOICE OF
RICHARD NIXON AND HIS DISTORTED FACE ON THE TV SCREEN

                    NIXON
          Sacrifice ... sacrifice ...
          sacrifice ...

DUKE PASSES OUT.

BLACK SCREEN

INT. FLAMINGO HOTEL SUITE — NIGHT

Darkness. Insanely, somewhere NILSSON plays — "Put the
lime in the coconut and mix em all up ..."

                    DUKE V/O
          What kind of rat-bastard psychotic
          would play that song — right now, at
          this moment?

DUKE opens his eyes and the hotel suite rushes in. He
lies, awkwardly twisted — unable to move. He could have
been there days — months.

                    DUKE V/O
        When I came to the general back alley
        ambience of the suite was so rotten,
        so incredibly foul. How long had I
        been lying there? Hours? Days?
        Months? All these signs of violence.
        What had happened?

DUKE moves his eyes — taking in his surroundings: Like
THE SIGHT OF SOME DISASTROUS ZOOLOGICAL EXPERIMENT involv-
ing whisky and gorillas. Blue and red Christmas tree
lights replace lightbulbs, used towels hanging everywhere,
pornographic pictures ripped out of a magazine are plas-
tered on a shattered mirror.

                    DUKE V/O
        There was evidence in this room of
        excessive consumption of almost every
        type of drug known to civilized man
        since 1544 AD.

DUKE manages to move — stiffly gets to his bare feet —
HOBBLES ROUND THE TRASHED ROOM like a newly risen ape.

                    DUKE V/O
        But what kind of addict would need
        all these coconut husks and crushed
        honeydew rinds? Would the presence of
        junkies account for all these uneaten
        french fries? These puddles of glazed
        ketchup on the bureau? Maybe so, but
        then why all this <u>booze</u>? And these
        crude pornographic photos smeared
        with mustard that had dried to a hard
        yellow crust ...

DUKE peers into Gonzo's room — HIS BED LIKE A BURNED OUT
RAT'S NEST — blackened springs and wires.

                    DUKE V/O
        These were not the hoof prints of
        your normal god-fearing junkie. It
        was too savage, too aggressive.

QUICK FLASHBACK:

GONZO SMASHES THE TEN FOOT MIRROR WITH A HAMMER!

BACK IN THE ROOM:

DUKE stares at the smashed mirror.

DUKE V/O
Grim memories and bad flashbacks.

In the bathroom, DUKE'S unlaced boots CRUSH BROKEN GLASS
IN VOMIT AND GRAPEFRUIT RINDS.

DUKE unzips and pisses. THERE IN THE TOILET BOWL IS THE
MAGNUM .357!

DUKE V/O
Something ugly had happened. I was
sure of it....

DUKE stares at the golden stream SPLASHING ON THE GUN.

The SOUNDS OF VOMITING come from a closet near the front
door.

DUKE looks into the room. He sees GONZO's ass sticking
out of the closet. He opens his mouth to speak when, IN
THE SMASHED MIRROR HE SEES THE FRAGMENTED REFLECTION OF
HIMSELF ... sleeping on the sofa.

The ominous SOUND OF A KEY TURNING in the room lock.

A hellish scream wakes up the SLEEPING DUKE. He sees
GONZO grappling naked with the maid — gun to her head.
GONZO is muffling her screams with an ice bag.

MAID
Please ... please ... I'm only the
maid. I didn't mean nothin!...

DUKE
(jumps up from the bed,
flashing his press badge)
YOU'RE UNDER ARREST!

GONZO
(to DUKE)
She must have used a pass key. I was
polishing my shoes in the closet when
I noticed her sneaking in—so I took
her.

DUKE shakes his head.

                    DUKE
              (barks at the MAID)
What made you do it? Who paid you
off?

                    MAID
Nobody. I'm the <u>maid</u>!

                    GONZO
You're lying! You were after the evi-
dence. Who put you up to this — the
manager?

                    MAID
I don't know what you're talking
about!

                    GONZO
Bullshit! You're just as much a part
of it as they are!

                    MAID
Part of w<u>hat?</u>

                    DUKE
The dope ring. You must know what's
going on in this hotel. Why do you
think we're here?

                    MAID
              (blubbering)
I know you're cops, but I thought you
were just here for that convention. I
swear! All I wanted to do was clean
up the room. I don't know anything
about <u>dope</u>!

GONZO laughs.

                    GONZO
Come on, baby don't try to tell us
you never heard of the Grange Gorman.

                    MAID
No! No! I swear to Jesus I never
heard of that stuff!

                    DUKE
Maybe she's telling the truth. Maybe

                    185

she's <u>not</u> <u>part</u> of it.

                    MAID
No! I swear I'm not!

                    GONZO
              (long pause)
In that case, maybe she can help.

                    MAID
Yes! I'll help you all you need! I
<u>hate</u> dope!

                    DUKE
So do we, lady.

                    GONZO
              (helping her up)
I think we should put her on the pay-
roll. See what she comes up with.

                    DUKE
Do you think you can handle it?

                    MAID
What?

                    GONZO
One phone call every day. Just tell
us what you've seen. Don't worry if
it doesn't add up, that's <u>our</u> problem.

GONZO hustles the MAID to the door.

                    MAID
You'd <u>pay</u> me for that?

                    DUKE
You're damn right. But the first time
you say anything about this, to <u>any-</u>
<u>body</u> — you'll go straight to prison
for the rest of your life. What's
your name?

                    MAID
Alice. Just ring Linen Service and
ask for Alice.

                    GONZO
Alright, Alice ... you'll be contact-
ed by Inspector Rock. Arthur Rock.
He'll be posing as a policitian.

                    DUKE
Inspector Rock will pay you. In cash.
A thousand dollars on the ninth of
every month.

                    MAID
Oh Lord! I'd do just about anything
for that!

                    GONZO
You and a lot of other people.

                    DUKE
The password is: "One Hand Washes The
Other." The minute you hear that, you
say "I fear nothing."

                    MAID
I fear nothing.

She repeats the password several times while they listen
to make sure she has it right.

                    GONZO
Oh, and don't bother to make up the
room. That way we won't have to risk
another of these little incidents,
will we?

                    MAID
Whatever you say, gentlemen. I can't
tell you how sorry I am about what
happened ...

                    GONZO
Don't worry, it's all over now. Thank
God for the decent people.

She smiles, repeating to herself "One Hand Washes The
Other" as GONZO hangs the DO NOT DISTURB sign and shuts
the door.

CUT BACK TO THE PRESENT.

A grimy tape runs through a grunged-up portable tape
recorder

GONZO ON TAPE
... Thank God for the <u>decent</u> people.

DUKE sits in the middle of the wrecked suite with his
mangled tape recorder in front of him.

DUKE V/O
Memories of that night are extremely
hazy ...

DUKE fast forwards through the tape — SEARCHING: *"Awwww,*
mama..can this really..be the end...?"

[**TACO STAND. OMITTED SCENE**]

EXT. SAFEWAY SUPERMARKET — DAY.

The WHITE WHALE waits — gleaming — beautiful.

DUKE V/O
There is a definite obligation, when
you boom around Vegas in a white
Coupe de Ville, to maintain a certain
style.

DUKE and GONZO burst out of the supermarket riding a
shopping basket loaded with COCONUTS, GRAPEFRUIT and
TEQUILLA. They send DEFEATED SHOPPERS sprawling.

The trolley collides into the WHITE WHALE. SHOPPERS gather
at the supermarket entrance to watch — baskets loaded with
junk, SCREAMING KIDS and EMPTY WALLETS.

DUKE switches on the music: JUMPING JACK FLASH. He selects
a coconut — ceremonially balances it on the hood. GONZO
pulls out a silver claw-hammer. A sly look at the gathering CROWD ... then he smashes the hammer down on the
coconut!

A GASP from the surly SHOPPERS.

DUKE places another coconut. SMASH! Milk and white meat
flies everywhere.

                    SHOPPER #1
        Hey! Is that your car?

                       DUKE
        Sure is.

SMASH! Coconut fragments fly.

                       DUKE
        Any of your folks want the milk?
        We're after the meat. This is honest
        coconut essence. Real meat.

SMASH!

                    SHOPPER #2
        Meat, hell! Look what you're doing to
        that car!

                      GONZO
        Fuck the car. They should make these
        things with a goddamn FM radio.

SMASH!

                       DUKE
        Yeh ... This foreign made crap — is
        sucking our dollar balance dry!

                    SHOPPER #3
        Someone should stop them!

SMASH!

                       DUKE
        You poor fools don't understand, do
        you? This car is the property of the
        World Bank! That money goes to ITALY!

                    SHOPPER #3
        Somebody should call the police!

                      GONZO
        Police? Are you people crazy?

GONZO confronts the CROWD, hammer in one hand, a coconut
in the other.

                        189

GONZO (CONT'D)
        You folks ever heard of ole Patrick
        Henry? Know what he said?!

Silence — the CROWD uncomprehending of this STONE DEGENER-
ATE.

                    GONZO (CONT'D)
                       (ROARS)
        GIVE ME LIBERTY OR GIVE ME DEATH!

GONZO brings the hammer down on the hood. CLANG!

A gasp from the CROWD. Getting ugly.

                    GONZO (CONT'D)
        In Samoa we LOVE THE CONSTITUTION!

                    SHOPPER #2
        Bullshit.

The CROWD move in.

                    SHOPPER #1
        Call the goddamn police!

GONZO SWINGS THE HAMMER. CLANG!

                    SHOPPER #4
        Look what they've done to that beau-
        tiful car!

DUKE jumps in behind the wheel.

                    DUKE
        This crowd is not rational. They
        can't relate to us. Let's go!

A final CLANG! GONZO jumps in.

DUKE floors the accelarator — screams at the CROWD.

                    DUKE
        You people voted for Hubert Humphrey!
        You killed Jesus!

They swerve round and through the CROWD.

                    DUKE V/O
        The crowd broke ranks. Nobody wants

to be run over by a Coupe de Ville.

INT. HOTEL FLAMINGO SUITE — NIGHT

DUKE FAST-FORWARDS ... PLAYS THE TAPE ...

> **VOICE ON TAPE**
> You <u>found</u> the American Dream? In <u>this</u>
> town?

> **DUKE ON TAPE**
> We're sitting on the main nerve <u>right</u>
> <u>now</u> ...

INT. BAZOOKO CIRCUS REVOLVING BAR — NIGHT

DUKE and GONZO (wearing a single black glove) talk con-
spiratorially to a 3RD MAN. A PLACID ORANGUTAN in a bow
tie sits next to him. THE BAR IS REVOLVING FASTER THAN
NORMAL. DUKE IS INSANELY TALKATIVE — WIRED!

> **DUKE**
> The manager told me a story about the
> owner of this place ... about how he
> always wanted to run away and join
> the circus when he was a kid. Well,
> now the bastard has his own circus,
> and a license to steal, too.

> **3RD MAN**
> You're right — he's the model.

> **DUKE**
> Absolutely! Pure Horatio Alger ...
> Say ...

INT. FLAMINGO HOTEL SUITE — NIGHT

DUKE playing the tape.

> **DUKE ON TAPE**
> ... how much do you think he'd take
> for the ape?

DUKE fast-forwards again — searching ... TRAFFIC NOISES.
SCREECH OF BRAKES.

> **VOICE ON TAPE**
> Holy God!...

A TERRIBLE GRINDING NOISE.

EXT. CAR RENTAL AGENCY — NIGHT

                    RENTAL AGENT
          Holy God!, how did this happen?

                        DUKE
          They beat the shit out of it.

                    RENTAL AGENT
          The top's completely jammed!

The CAR RENTAL AGENT wrestles with the trashed car.

                        DUKE
          Yeah, something's wrong with the
          motor....

INT. FLAMINGO HOTEL SUITE — NIGHT

                    DUKE ON TAPE
           ... The generator light's been on
          red ever since I drove the thing into
          Lake Mead on a water test ...

A HUGE SPLASH ...

The tape's gone too far.

                        DUKE
              No, no. Shit ...

DUKE races the tape BACKWARDS... Then, SIRENS HOWL.

                    DUKE ON TAPE
          Where's the ape? I'm ready to write a
          check.

INT. BAZOOKO CIRCUS BAR — NIGHT

DUKE is standing in the middle of A SEMI-DESTROYED BAZOOKO
CIRCUS REVOLVING BAR. Mirrors are broken. People are
recovering from some kind of battle. THE BAR SPINS MADLY.
DUKE IS INSANELY WIRED.

                        3RD MAN
          Forget it, he just attacked an old
          man...he took a bite out of the bar-

tender's <u>head</u>! The cops took the ape
away.

DUKE

Goddamnit! What's the bail? I <u>want</u>
that ape! I've already reserved two
first-class seats on the plane.

DUKE V/O

There was every reason to believe
that we had been heading for trouble,
that we'd pushed our luck a bit
far...

EXT. WHITE WHALE ON THE STREETS OF LAS VEGAS — NIGHT

GONZO SCREAMS ABUSE out of the window at a Ford alongside
the VOMIT STREAKED WHITE WHALE. DUKE MAKES A SUPERHUMAN
EFFORT TO STAY ON THE ROAD.

GONZO

Hey there! You folks want to buy some
heroin?

In the Ford: TWO COUPLES — MIDDLE AGED AMERICAN FACES
FROZEN IN SHOCK — stare straight ahead. GONZO leans out —
close to them.

GONZO

Hey, honkies! Goddamnit, I'm serious.
I want to sell you some pure fucking
smack!

No reaction.

GONZO

Cheap heroin! This is the real stuff!
You won't get hooked. I just got back
from Vietnam! This is scag, folks.
Pure scag!

The lights change. The Ford bolts. DUKE keeps pace with
them.

GONZO

Shoot! Fuck! Scag! Blood! Heroin!
Rape! Cheap! Communist! Jab it right
in your fucking eyeballs!

The MAN IN THE BACK SEAT suddenly loses control —
enraged, lunges against the glass, trying to get at GONZO.

>   **MAN IN CAR**
>   You dirty bastards! Pull over and
>   I'll kill you! God damn you! You bas-
>   tards!

INT. FLAMINGO HOTEL SUITE — NIGHT

BACK IN THE SUITE:

The tape runs:

>   **MAN IN CAR ON TAPE**
>   You dirty bastards!

An ugly squeal of brakes.

>   **GONZO ON TAPE**
>   Shit, he was trying to bite me! I
>   shoulda maced the fucker!

DUKE fast forwards the tape. The TAPE MANGLES — the
sounds skid to a halt....

DUKE grabs the nearest tool — uses it to hook out the
tape, then realizes... IT'S GONZO'S RAZOR-SHARP FOLDING
KNIFE... A CHILLING MOMENT....

DUKE turns the knife over ... THERE'S A DRIED CRIMSON
SPOT ON THE BLADE ... OR IS IT DRIED MASHED POTATOES?
READ ON TO FIND OUT!

>   **DUKE**
>   (remembering)
>   Back door beauty!

>   **DUKE V/O**
>   The mentality of Las Vegas is so
>   grossly atavistic that a really mas-
>   sive crime often slips by unrecog-
>   nized.

DUKE SCRAPES A LITTLE OF THE CRUST — TASTES IT...

>   **DUKE V/O (CONT'D)**
>   The possibility of physical and men-
>   tal collapse is very real ... No

sympathy for the devil; keep that
in mind. Buy the ticket, take the
ride ...

HE HEARS THE SOUNDS OF SOMEONE BEING BEATEN UP...

VOICE OFF
Shit! Faggot! Bastard!

EXT. NORTH STAR COFFEE LOUNGE — NIGHT

WHACK! SHADOWY FIGURES beat up a MAN — give him A GOOD
KICKING. BRUTAL AND UGLY.

DUKE V/O
North Vegas is where you go when
you've fucked up once too often on
The Strip and when you're not even
welcome in the cut-rate Downtown
places.

PAN to reveal a seedy diner — THE NORTH STAR CAFE in the
background. Through the window — DUKE and GONZO sit at
the counter.

INT. NORTH STAR COFFEE LOUNGE — NIGHT

DUKE V/O
The North Star Coffee Lounge seemed
like a fairly safe haven from our
storms. No hassles, no talk. Just a
place to rest and regroup. I wasn't
even hungry.

GONZO stuffs a hamburger down PAYING NO ATTENTION TO THE
BEATING going on outside the window. Duke reads a newspa-
per.

DUKE V/O
There was nothing in the atmosphere
of the North Star to put me on my
guard...
GONZO
                    (to WAITRESS)
Two glasses of ice water with ice.

The WAITRESS brings the ice water.

                          DUKE V/O
              She looked like a burnt out carica-
              ture of Jane Russell. She was defi-
              nitely in charge here....

GONZO gulps down his glass of water and hands her a napkin.

                          DUKE V/O
              He did it very casually, but I knew
              that our peace was about to be shat-
              tered.

                          DUKE
              What was that?

GONZO shrugs.

The WAITRESS stands at the end of the counter with her
back to them while she ponders the napkin.... She turns.

                          WAITRESS
              What is this?

                          GONZO
              A napkin.

THE WAITRESS slams the napkin down on the counter.

                          WAITRESS
              Don't give me that bullshit! I know
              what it means! You goddamn fat pimp
              bastard.

                          GONZO
              That's the name of a horse I used to
              own. What's wrong with you?

                          WAITRESS
              You sonofabitch! I take a lot of shit
              in this place, but I sure as hell
              don't have to take it off a SPIC
              PIMP!

GONZO GOES VERY VERY STILL AT THIS ...

                          DUKE V/O
              Jesus, I thought, what's happening?

DUKE picks up the napkin. On it is printed in careful red
letters: "BACK DOOR BEAUTY?"

> ### DUKE V/O (CONT'D)
> The question mark was emphasized.

> ### WAITRESS
> (screams)
> Pay your bill and get the hell out!
> You want me to call the cops?

> ### GONZO
> Spic pimp?

GONZO's hand goes inside his shirt. He PULLS OUT THE
RAZOR-SHARP HUNTING KNIFE.

GONZO KEEPS HIS EYES ON THE WAITRESS. He walks about six
feet down the aisle and lifts the receiver of the pay
phone. He SLICES IT OFF, then brings the receiver back to
his stool and sits down.

> ### DUKE V/O
> I was stupid with shock — not knowing
> whether to run or start laughing.

> ### GONZO
> (casual)
> How much is the lemon meringue pie?

> ### DUKE V/O
> Her eyes were turgid with fear, but
> her brain was functioning on some
> basic motor survival level.

> ### WAITRESS
> (blurting — on automatic)
> Thirty-five cents!

> ### GONZO
> (laughing)
> I mean the whole pie.

The WAITRESS MOANS. GONZO places a $5 BILL on the
counter.

> ### GONZO
> Let's say five dollars. Okay?

GONZO walks round the counter TAKING THE PIE OUT OF THE
DISPLAY CASE.

> **DUKE V/O**
> The sight of the blade had triggered
> bad memories. The glazed look in her
> eyes said her throat had been cut.
> She was still in the grip of paraly-
> sis when we left.

DUKE IS ROOTED TO THE SPOT.

GONZO urges him out the door. The camera retreats with
them.

The WAITRESS STANDS THERE — PETRIFIED. Alone in a lousy
bar at night.

INT. FLAMINGO HOTEL SUITE — NIGHT

DUKE's face as he stares at the knife — remembering ...

> **GONZO V/O**
> Drive! Drive! Drive! We have fifteen
> fucking minutes to get me on that
> plane!

EXT. ROAD ON OUTSKIRTS OF LAS VEGAS — DAY

The WHITE WHALE, looking like shit - it's TOP HALF UP,
TORN, SLAPPING IN THE WIND - ROARS THROUGH AN INTERSECTION
as the light turns red.

DR.GONZO FRANTICALLY PAWS OVER A MAP.

DUKE drives — SILENT AND FURIOUS — sick to his stomach
with the PSYCHOTIC GONZO.

> **GONZO**
> What are you doing? You were supposed
> to turn back there!

> **DUKE V/O**
> We had abused every rule that Vegas
> lived by — burning the locals, abus-
> ing the tourists, terrifying the
> help. The only chance now, I felt,
> was the possibility that we'd gone to
> such excess that nobody in the posi-

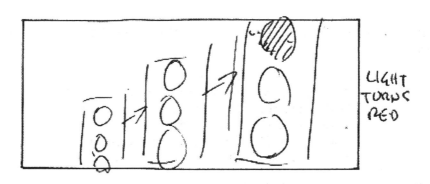

LIGHT
TURNS
RED

Duke
Punishing
Gonzo

1SI cut after North Star

WHEEL
SKIDDING
TO STOP

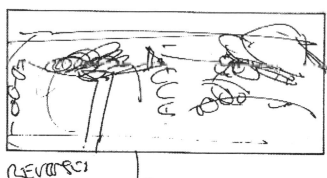

CAR REVERSES

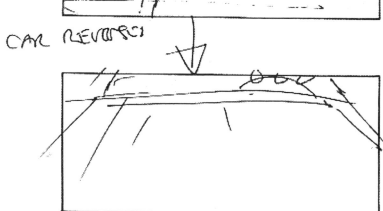

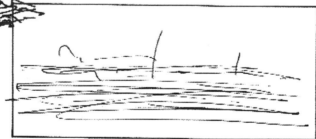

TRACKING — BLURRED LANDSCAPE

WHALE ENTERS

BLURRED
YELLOW
LINE

> tion to bring the hammer down on us
> could possibility believe it.

DUKE suddenly SLAMS ON THE BRAKES.

> ### GONZO
> Jesus Christ!!!

There, crossing the road in front of them, is LUCY - her
paintings under her arm - looking lost. SHE LOOKS UP WITH
A VAGUE SENSE OF RECOGNITION ...

DUKE throws the car into A SKIDDING REVERSE TURN AND
ROARS OFF.

EXT. DESERT ROAD OUTSIDE LAS VEGAS — DAY

THE WHITE WHALE TEARS DOWN THE DESERTED FREEWAY. GONZO
looks wildly around.

> ### GONZO
> Goddamnit! We're lost! What are we
> doing out here on this godforsaken
> road?

GONZO sees that THEY'RE RUNNING PARALLEL WITH THE AIRPORT
RUNWAY.

> ### GONZO
> The airport is over there!

> ### DUKE
> Never missed a plane yet.

DUKE HITS THE BRAKES and wrenches the wheel — takes the
WHALE down into the grassy freeway divider. WHEELS CHURN-
ING, HE MAKES IT UP THE OPPOSITE BANK, nose of the car
straight up, then BOUNCES ONTO THE FREEWAY and keeps going
right OVER A FENCE, dragging it through a cactus field
and onto the RUNWAY.

GONZO is FROZEN WITH FEAR — GRIPPING THE DASHBOARD. He
throws a worried look at DUKE.

> ### DUKE
> I'll drop you right next to the
> plane.

They SPEED UNDER A PARKED AIRPLANE, SHOUTING ABOVE THE JET

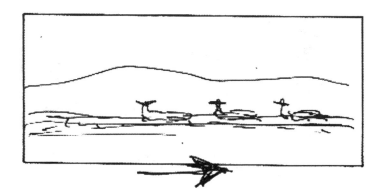

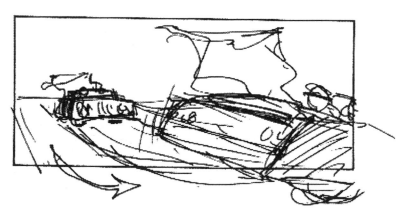

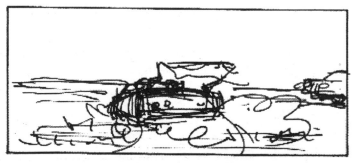

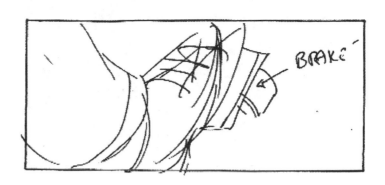

BRAKE

WHEEL TURN - POV

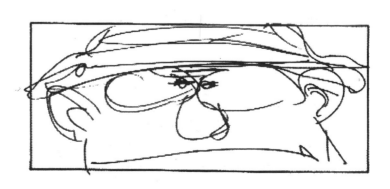

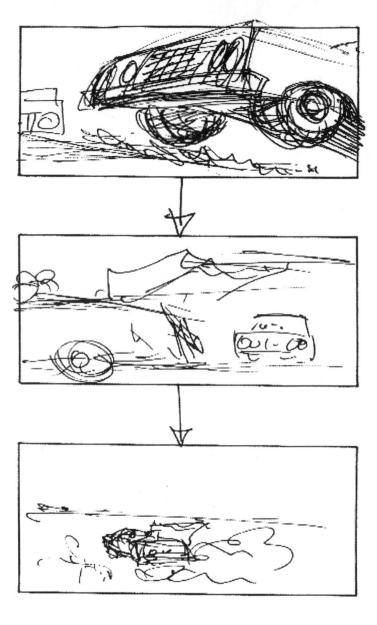

JIGGLE MOOUT

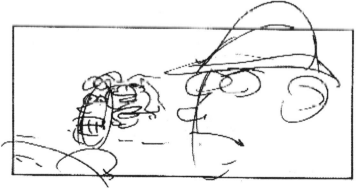

TUMBLE WEEDS

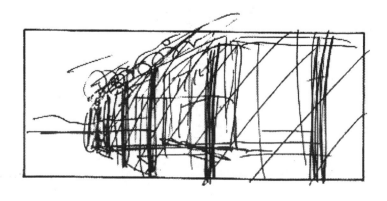

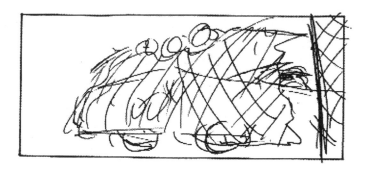

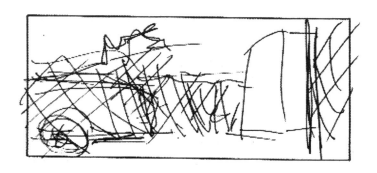

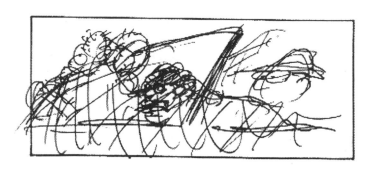

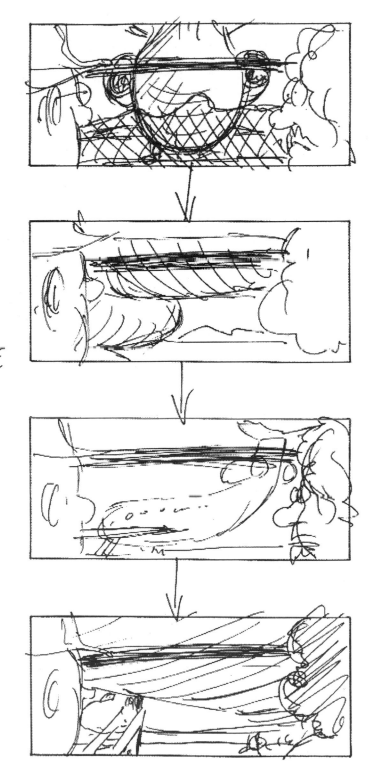

DO
ONE
CLEAN
POV
of
RIDE

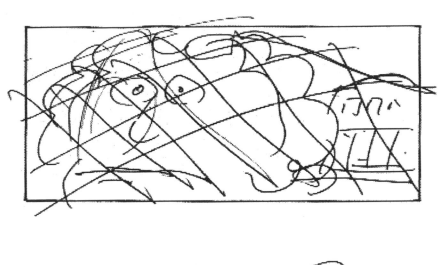

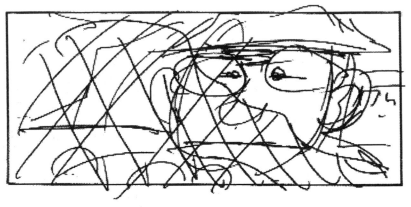

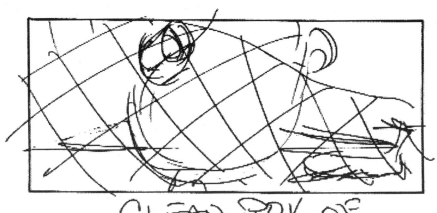

CLEAN POV OF
RIDE TO PLANE

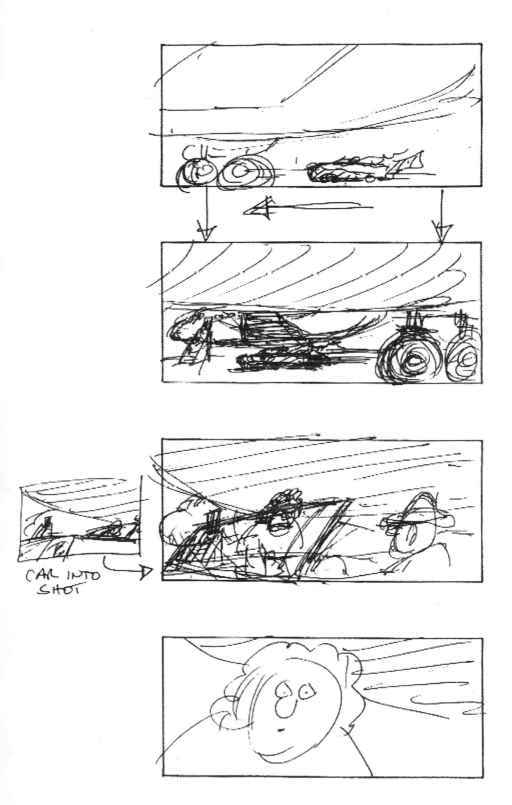

CAR INTO
SHOT

c/u

ENGINE SCREAM.

> GONZO
> No! I can't get out! They'll crucify
> me. I'll have to take the blame!

> DUKE
> (irritatedly)
> Ridiculous! Just say you were hitch-
> hiking to the airport and I picked
> you up. You never saw me before.
> Shit, this town is full of white
> Cadillac convertibles. I plan too go
> through there so fast that nobody
> will even glimpse the goddamn licence
> plate. You ready?

> GONZO
> Why not? But for Christ's sake, just
> do it fast!

EXT. AT THE AIRPLANE — DAY

DUKE SCREECHES UP in front of the DESERT AIR 727. GONZO
JUMPS OUT — HEADS FOR THE PLANE.

DUKE watches him go — RELENTS.

> DUKE
> Hey!

GONZO stops - turns.

> DUKE
> Don't take any guff from those swine.
> Remember, if you have any trouble you
> can always send a telegram to the
> Right People.

> GONZO
> Yeah... Explaining my Position. Some
> asshole wrote a poem about that
> once...

GONZO pauses.

> GONZO
> Probably good advice, if you have
> shit for brains.

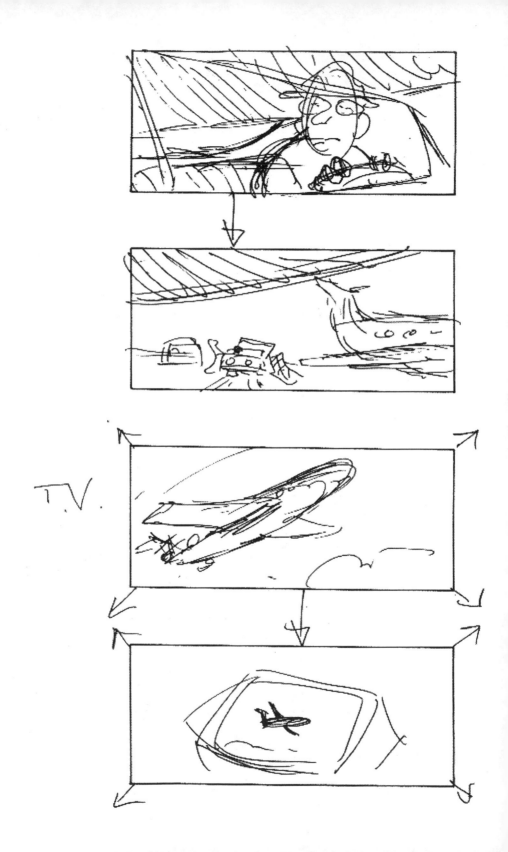

T.V.

GONZO turns and RACES TOWARD THE STEPS JUST AS HE IS
ABOUT TO ENTER THE PLANE HE PAUSES AND LOOKS
BACK..SMILES.. AND LEANS FORWARD AND VOMITS.

> **DUKE V/O**
> There he goes — one of God's own pro-
> totypes — a high powered mutant of
> some kind never even considered for
> mass production. Too weird to live
> and too rare to die.

DUKE watches for a second then ROARS AWAY. PULL BACK WITH
THE WHITE SHARK — LEAVING THE AIRPLANE FAR BEHIND.

INT FLAMINGO HOTEL SUITE/APOCALYPSE — NIGHT

On the TV an airplane soars thru the sky. Pull back to
find DUKE barricaded in GONZO'S BEDROOM. He is typing on
his typewriter.

> **DUKE**
> We are all wired into a survival trip

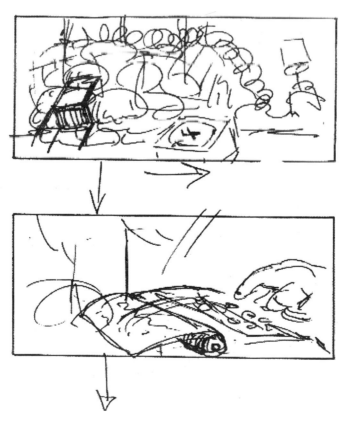

215

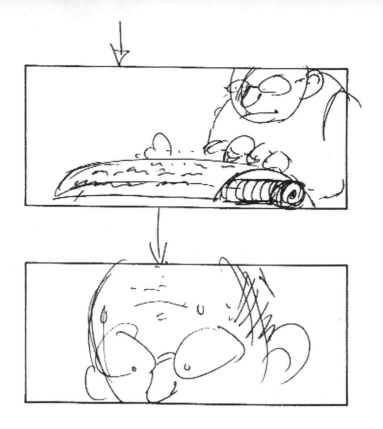

now. No more of the speed that fueled
the 60's. That was the fatal flaw in
Tim Leary's trip. He crashed around
America selling "consciousness expan-
sion" without ever giving a thought
to the grim meat-hook realities that
were lying in wait for all the people
who took him seriously....

DUKE records like A WAR CORRESPONDENT. The CAMERA slowly
rises — DUKE alone in the room with the TV SPEWING OUT
IMAGES OF WARS AND CIVIL UNREST OF THE 90's.

DUKE

All those pathetically eager acid
freaks who thought they could buy
Peace and Understanding for three
bucks a hit. But their loss and fail-
ure is ours too. What Leary took down
with him was the central illusion of
a whole life-style that he helped
create....

RISING HIGHER — THE WALLS OF THE ROOM APPEAR TO BE 20 TO

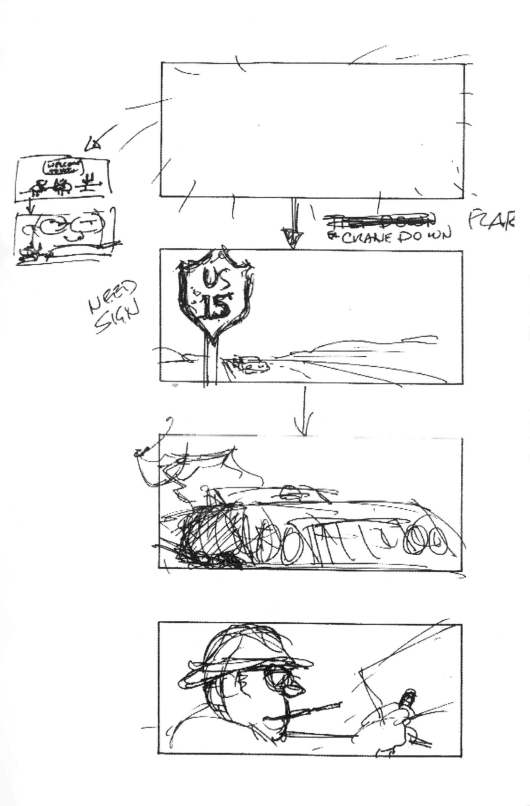

CRANE DOWN

PLAR

NEED
SIGN

US
15

30 FEET HIGH. DUKE SEEMS TO BE AT THE BOTTOM OF A WELL...
THE CAMERA RISES UP THROUGH BROKEN TIMBERS ...

                        DUKE
            ... a generation of permanent crip-
            ples, failed seekers, who never
            understood the essential old-mystic
            fallacy of the Acid Culture: the des-
            perate assumption that somebody... or
            at least some force — is tending the
            light at the end of the tunnel.

HIGHER STILL — DUKE ALONE IN THE ROOM — AN ISOLATED BOX
SURROUNDED BY THE TWISTED METAL AND RUBBLE AND SMASHED
NEON SIGNS OF THE DEAD CITY — A BLASTED LANDSCAPE WITHOUT
LIGHT — SHARDS OF A CIVILIZATION.

EXT. DESERT HIGHWAY — DAY

A BURNING FLARED-OUT SUN. The camera pans down to DUKE
DRIVING THE WRECKED WHALE. A piece of the fence flies out
of the back seat as he takes a bump.

                     DUKE V/O
            There was only one road back to L.A.
            US Interstate 15, just a flat-out
            high speed burn through Baker and
            Barstow and Berdoo, then on to the
            Hollywood Freeway straight into fran-
            tic oblivion: safety, obscurity, just
            another freak in the Freak Kingdom.

DUKE sees THE HARDWARE BARN, A RUSTIC OLD FARM BUILDING
facing the road with a single gas pump outside and a neon
sign that flashes beer.

                        DUKE
            Ahhh. Wonderful.

DUKE PULLS OFF THE ROAD and parks. Gets out and walks in.

INT. HARDWARE BARN - BAKER, CALIFORNIA — DAY

DUKE enters the DARK, CLUTTERED INTERIOR. Scattered all
about the store are BITS OF AMERICANA... OLD BARRELS,
WAGON WHEELS, WOODEN YOKES. A STUFFED HORSE HANGS FROM THE
RAFTERS. The sunlight shafts through high windows. AN OLD
MAN is repairing an iron pot-bellied stove near the wooden
bar. A NORMAN ROCKWELL PAINTING... ONLY REAL.

                    PROPRIETOR
        What'll you have?

DUKE can't quite believe this place — too good to be
true.

                       DUKE
                    (doubtfully)
        Ballantine Ale ...?

THE PROPRIETOR serves the ale up ice cold. DUKE SMILES
AND RELAXES.

                       DUKE
        Hard to find it served like this any-
        more.

As he drinks, DUKE toys with a rack of key chains — LIT-
TLE AMERICAN ICONS ... A REMINGTON COWBOY, A BUGS BUNNY,
A TWEETY PIE, BETTY BOOP, A BASEBALL PLAYER. The logo on
the rack reads: AMERICAN DREAM KEY RINGS.

                    PROPRIETOR
        Where ya comin' from, young man?

                       DUKE
        Las Vegas.

                    PROPRIETOR
        A great town, that Vegas. I bet you
        had good luck there. You're the type.

                       DUKE
        I know. I'm a triple Scorpio.

                    PROPRIETOR
                    (trustingly)
        That's a fine combination. You can't
        lose.

A LOVELY GIRL appears. Seeing DUKE, she smiles. CAN THIS
REALLY BE HIS LUCKY DAY? She approaches him.... and.....
KISSES THE PROPRIETOR.

                       DUKE
                (caught off guard ... mutter-
                            ing)
        Oh, my God!...

                        220

                    PROPRIETOR
                  (not understanding)
          This is my granddaughter....

                       DUKE
                     (recovering}
          Don't worry....
                  (leans forward in
                     confidence)
          ... and I'm actually the District
          Attorney from Ignoto County.
                      (winks)
          Just another good American like your-
          self.

A MOMENT. THE PROPRIETOR'S SMILE DISAPPEARS.

Wordlessly the PROPRIETOR and his GRANDDAUGHTER go to the
back of the store — GET ON WITH THEIR WORK — IGNORING
DUKE.

WHO FEELS ASHAMED.

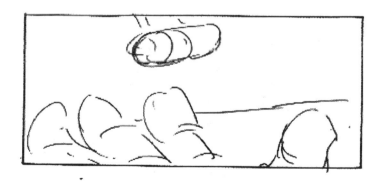

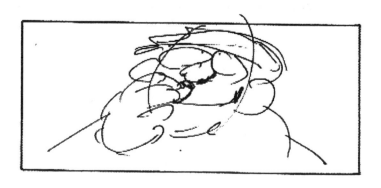

DUKE puts some money down on the bar and SLOWLY LEAVES.

EXT. HARDWARE BARN — DAY

A CHASTENED DUKE approaches the vomit streaked WHITE
WHALE. Gets in — sits there — deflated — miserable...

A state bus draws up across from the Hardware Barn.

Sombrely, DUKE watches as TWO YOUNG MARINES with duffel
bags step off — chatting like TRUE BROTHERS...

DUKE switches on the ignition. Something rolls off the
trembling dash.... DUKE catches it....

ONE SINGLE BEAUTIFUL AMYL CAPSULE ...

DUKE CRACKS THE AMYL - INHALES. THE RUSH MAKES HIM GASP -
TEETH BARED LIKE A MADMAN.

                              DUKE
                HOLY SHIT!!!

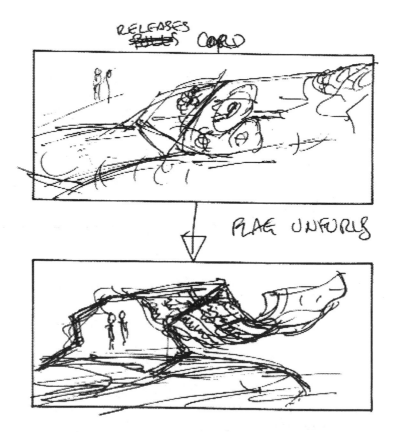

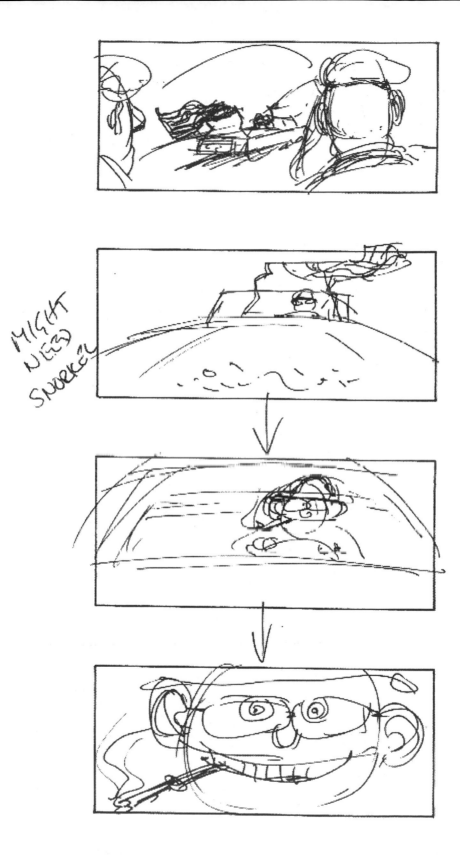

MIGHT
NEED
SNORKEL

DUKE GUNS THE ENGINE with a laugh — leans out — YELLS AT
THE MARINES.

DUKE
GOD'S MERCY ON YOU SWINE!

DUKE ROARS AWAY. AN AMERICAN FLAG FLIES UP FROM THE
DEBRIS IN THE BACK SEAT, MADLY UNFURLING ITSELF AS IT
SNAGS ON THE CONVERTIBLE-TOP FRAME OF THE TRASHED WHITE
WHALE!

AAAAAAAARRRRRRRRRRRRRRRRRGGGGGGGGGGGHHHHHH!!!!!!!!!

The TWO MARINES look after him CONFUSED.

EXT. DESERT HIGHWAY

DUKE drives fast — TEETH GRITTED IN FROZEN ECSTASY!!

DUKE CRANKS UP THE TAPE RECORDER.

DUKE V/O
My heart was filled with joy.
I felt like a monster reincarnation

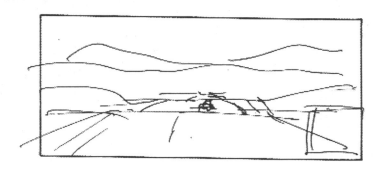

of Horatio Alger ... a man on
the move... and just sick
enough to be totally confident.

The WHITE WHALE WIPES THE SCREEN BLACK.

AAAAAAAARRRRRRRRRRRRRRRGGGGGGGGGGHHHHHH!!!!!!!!!

END

LOSING THE

LIGHT

TERRY GILLIAM AND THE MUNCHAUSEN SAGA

BY ANDREW YULE

"A WICKEDLY FUNNY RECOUNTING ... Mix one American director with a German producer on a period extravaganza, set the locations in Italy and Spain and start the cameras rolling without enough money to do the job. Then sit back and watch disaster strike. That is the scenario Andrew Yule has recounted in LOSING THE LIGHT...[He] has painstakingly reconstructed the making in 1987 and 1988 of The Adventures of Baron Munchausen ... The more problems and reverses, the greater our interest ... costly postponements ... overwhelming language difficulties, elephants and tigers turning on their trainers, illnesses, sets not being ready, special effects breaking down and cameo stars (from Marlon Brando to Sean Connery) backing out of the project. You name it, Mr. Yule reports it ..."

— DANIEL SELZNICK
THE NEW YORK TIMES BOOK REVIEW

ISBN 1–55783–346-X • $15.95 • PAPERBACK

THE ADVENTURES OF BARON MUNCHAUSEN

THE ILLUSTRATED SCREENPLAY
by Terry Gilliam & Charles McKeown

*"A carnival! A wonderland! A weekend with nine Friday nights! Terry Gilliam's **LAVISH DREAMS** are beyond those of mere mortals."*
— HARLAN ELLISON

*"Truly **ASTONISHING** ... "*
— JACK KROLL, *NEWSWEEK*

*" ... the spectacle is **SPECTACULAR** ... "*
— VINCENT CANBY
THE NEW YORK TIMES

Baron Munchausen, one of the most famous liars in history, first recounted his adventures over two hundred years ago and since then they have been retold and added to by storytellers around the world.

The original *Adventures*, written by Rudolph Erich Raspe in 1785, became an instant best-seller, and was hailed as a comic sensation in the satirical spirit of *Gulliver's Travels* and *Tom Jones*. Terry Gilliam has now resurrected the Baron and his comrades in a volume destined to be a classic for generations to come.

ISBN: 1-55783-041-X • $8.95 • paper

THE FISHER KING

THE BOOK OF THE FILM
by Richard LaGravanese,
Introduction by Terry Gilliam

"FOUR STARS. A bold, unique and exhilarating cinematic trip. An astonishing comedy about love, loss, and redemption. **FISHER KING** *SOARS!"*
— BRUCE WILLIAMSON, *PLAYBOY*

"One of the year's best films! **WITTY, WISE, INTELLECTUAL, AND TOTALLY UNPREDICTABLE.**"
— JEFFREY LYONS, *SNEAK PREVIEWS*

"THE FISHER KING takes enormous risks and pulls off the challenge ... Gilliam's most satisfying film."
— JOAN BUCK, *VOGUE*

Special Features of the Applause edition:

- Extensive interviews with Terry Gilliam and Robin Williams

- The complete final draft shooting script in professional screenwriter's format

- Over 200 photos for the film

- An afterword by the screenwriter, Richard LaGravenese, detailing the writing and production history of the film

- An annotated appendix of deleted or altered scenes, illustrating the evolution of the final film

---

ISBN: 1-55783-098-3 • $12.95 • paperback

A FISH CALLED WANDA

by John Cleese and Charles Crichton

*"The **FUNNIEST** movie this year!"*

— ROGER EBERT,
SISKEL & EBERT

"Wanda defies gravity, in both senses of the work, and ***REDEFINES A GREAT COMIC TRADITION.***

— RICHARD SCHICKEL, *TIME*

*"**WANDA** Is wonderful ... I fell for it hook, line and sinker. The script is **HYSTERICAL.**"*

— JOEL SIEGEL, ABC–TV

*"The **MEANEST,** most consistently hysterical film in ages ... the writing is sharply pointed and delightfully Irreverent."*

— MARSHALL FINE
GANNETT NEWSPAPERS

"OUTRAGEOUSLY OUTSTANDING!"

— DENNIS CUNNINGHAM, CBS–TV

1-55783-033-9 • Paperback • $8.95

JFK:
The Book of the Film
By Oliver Stone and Zachary Sklar

Applause is proud to present the documented screenplay of the most talked about film of the year, complete with over 300 resaerch notes by Oliver Stone.

This thorough and complete volume also includes lengthy excerpts from the JFK debate: over 200 pages of articles by such esteemed writers and commentators as Norman Mailer, Tom Wicker, Gerald Ford and others.

"JFK: The Book of the Film is **AN IMPORTANT RECORD OF AN UNPRECEDENTED MOMENT IN FILM HISTORY."**—Christopher Sharrett, *Cineaste*

ISBN: 1-55783-127-0 $18.95 trade paper